MANNERS of the HEART
At The Table

By

Jill Rigby Garner

Contributing Author, Shawna Gose, MS

Baton Rouge, LA

Published by MANNERS of the **HEART**®
215 Royal Street
Baton Rouge, Louisiana 70802
225.383.3235
www.mannersoftheheart.org

Copyright 2012, 2013 © by MANNERS of the **HEART**®

All rights reserved. Reprinted with revisions 2013.
Printed in the United States of America.

Graphic Design: Ashley Daigle
Cover Design: Brian Rivet

MANNERS of the **HEART**® grants teachers the right to photocopy the reproducibles from this book for classroom use. No other part of this book may be reproduced in whole or in part, or stored in a retrieval system, or transmitted in any form or by any means, electronic, mechanical, photocopying, recording or otherwise, without permission of the publisher.

Table of Contents

ACKNOWLEDGEMENTS..4
PREFACE 5
HOW TO USE THIS CURRICULUM 8

INTRODUCTION 12

- **CH. 1   TABLE TALK** 16
  USING GOOD CONVERSATION AT THE TABLE
- **CH. 2   FLATWARE GOES SOMEWHERE** 22
  SETTING THE TABLE
- **CH. 3   COME ONE, COME ALL** 29
  PREPARING FOR THE MEAL
- **CH. 4   MESS HALL MANNERS** 36
  COURTESY AND CONSIDERATION IN THE CAFETERIA
- **CH. 5   TOOLS OF THE TABLE** 43
  USING UTENSILS EFFICIENTLY
- **CH. 6   PASS THE PLATE, PLEASE** 50
  PASSING FOOD AT THE TABLE
- **CH. 7   BREAD, BUNS, BAGELS AND BISCUITS**..................56
  ENJOYING BREAD AND BUTTER
- **CH. 8   SPAGHETTI, SOUP AND OTHER TOUGH STUFF**..........61
  EATING DIFFICULT FOODS WITH EASE
- **CH. 9   CLEAR THE CLUTTER** 66
  END-OF-THE-MEAL REMINDERS
- **CH. 10 RESTAURANT RULES**.. 73
  EATING OUT IN PUBLIC PLACES

APPENDIX 80
- MASTERING MESSY MEALS.. 81
- ACTIVITIES & ATTRIBUTES CHART 82
- MATERIALS CHARTS 83
- WILBUR'S GLOSSARY 84

Acknowledgements

CONTRIBUTORS
Thank you to those who contributed to the creation of this curriculum: our local teachers, staff, consultants and friends:

Polly Allen
Katie Barker
Dawn Beale
Debbie Charbonnet
Katherine Chenevert
Melissa Hamel

Samantha McCartney
Jessica Neel
Chelsey Newnham
Lori Smith
Carter Stone
Lexi Verret

SPONSORS
Thank you to the foundations who sponsored the creation and piloting of this curriculum:

The Boo Grigsby Foundation
The Huey and Angelina Wilson Foundation
Blue Cross and Blue Shield of Louisiana Foundation
Albemarle Foundation
The Powell Group Fund

Preface

Can you imagine how different our classrooms would be if every child had *self-respect* and showed respect for others?

Wouldn't you enjoy a school environment filled with young people who were more concerned with what they could do for others rather than what others could do for them?

Manners know no social or cultural boundaries. Common courtesy and respect for others should be part of everyday living no matter where you live. Customs may differ from one region to another, from one side of town to another or from one country to another, but treating others with respect is a universal need. Defining manners as an attitude of the heart that is self-giving not self-serving, *Manners of the Heart* and *Manners of the Heart At the Table* teach children to respect others, and in the process, gain respect for themselves.

Manners of the Heart® was founded to help you help your students become respectful youngsters who grow up to become respectable adults. After more than ten years of working in schools, from the inner city to the suburbs, from the rural South to the affluent West Coast, we have identified the real problem that has plagued our educational system.

In the early '70s, specialists began telling us the secret to raising successful children was to build their self-esteem. Books on the subject skyrocketed to the top of best-seller lists, encouraging us to be friends with children, not authority figures. Discipline was out, praise was in. We stopped encouraging children to persevere until they achieved greatness. Instead, we told them they were the best just for *being*. Thus, the "sticker revolution" began, the idea that children deserve rewards for everything.

Here we are forty years later faced with plummeting test scores, escalating violence among even our youngest students, paralyzing entitlement and the highest drop-out rates in the history of our educational system. The evidence is clear—self-esteem is not the cure, but rather the culprit.

Preface

Manners of the Heart® has the solution. Heart education must be the foundation for education.

We don't tell children they're great; we help them become great. We don't tell children they're the best; we help them become their best. We don't teach children to do the right thing for a reward, but to do the right thing because it's the right thing to do. The outcome? Their self-esteem is replaced with self-respect and self-control.

During the early years of development of this curriculum, an astute principal at a neglected Mid-Atlantic school enlisted volunteers from her community to visit their cafeteria once a week to teach *Manners of the Heart At the Table*. The mayor, the grocer and the owner of the café all took turns. The pharmacist came. When the disc jockey of the local radio station came, the whole town heard about the plight of the school. By the end of the school year, the students had captured the hearts of their community's citizens.

Two retired carpenters volunteered to replace rotten wood around the school during the summer months. High school students cleaned and scrubbed long-forgotten windows. A paint brigade rolled in one day to freshen dull walls. Armed with gallons of paint, brushes and rollers, they painted walls and added a mural in the cafeteria to remind students to mind their manners.

When the next school year commenced, students and teachers returned to a school with the smells of new wood, freshly painted walls, and clean windows. Rather than feeling neglected, the students felt loved. The morale of the teachers improved. The students were motivated to work hard. Volunteers kept coming—reading, teaching, and caring. By the end of the next school year, new partnerships had formed. By the end of the following school year, academic scores were on the rise. The school experienced a rebirth!

And it all began with the introduction of *Manners of the Heart At the Table*.

Through *Manners of the Heart* and *Manners of the Heart At the Table*, schools experience a rise in academic scores, a decrease in disciplinary actions and greater parental and community involvement.

Preface

Improving academic scores begins with the belief there is more to education than science and math. Clarence Thomas, an Associate Justice of the Supreme Court, once said "Good manners will open doors that the best education cannot."[1] *Manners of the Heart At the Table* is here to help you help your students master social skills that will carry them from the classroom to the boardroom.

Manners of the Heart® stands with you in educating your students for life and living.

[1] www.goodreads.com

How to Use this Curriculum

Manners of the Heart At the Table is here to help you help your students. Together with our character education curriculum, this manual is designed to strengthen morals, improve social and emotional skills and increase respectfulness. *Manners of the Heart At the Table* is intended to develop your students' social skills, ultimately supporting their successful development in all areas of life. Believe it or not, your kids will enjoy learning table manners in this curriculum!

The results in your students will be the following:

- Increased prosocial attitudes and behaviors
- Enhanced sense of personal responsibility
- Increased self-regulated behavior
- Increased empathic ability
- Mastering of basic dining etiquette

The results in the classroom, home and community will be the following:

- Reduction in time spent managing disciplinary actions in the cafeteria
- Increased respectful student behavior inside and outside the cafeteria
- Enhanced ability to connect with students or children
- Increased pleasant dining experiences at the family dinner table
- Development of socially-aware community members

ORGANIZATION OF MANUAL

Manners of the Heart At the Table includes ten lessons for kindergarten through fifth-grade students. Each lesson is divided into classroom learning (10-15 minutes) and cafeteria learning (5-10 minutes/table). Each lesson additionally includes four or more **Extending Children's Learning** activities (5-15 minutes, depending on activity chosen) for daily reinforcement of the core principle and a **Home Connection** letter for parents.

The weekly lessons are organized as follows:

Attributes—Two or three traits the lesson instills in the heart of a child
Skills and Objectives—Grade-specific ideas the lesson teaches

How to Use this Curriculum

Materials and Preparation—A list of supplies or preparation needed and additional worksheets found in the manual

Wilbur's Words of Wisdom—A phrase or thought that offers the main teaching point

Guiding Children's Learning in the Classroom—Instructions to follow in the classroom portion of the lesson

Guiding Children's Learning in the Cafeteria—Instructions to follow in additional learning and reinforcement in the cafeteria

Extending Children's Learning—Four or more additional lessons to use each day of the week to reinforce the core lesson

Home Connection—A letter to send home to parents or guardians to keep them informed and engaged by offering further training for the child in the principles of the week's lesson

In *Manners of the Heart At the Table*, kindergarten through fifth-grade students receive the same lessons on table manners. There are several reasons for this:

- Children of all ages often eat in the cafeteria at the same time.
- Siblings of all ages are expected to display the same good manners at the table.
- Table manners need to be repeated and reinforced as children grow.
- The 'rules of etiquette' are the same from ages 5 to 105!

INSTRUCTIONAL SUGGESTIONS

Manners of the Heart At the Table is intended to be customized to the teaching environment of your school. This curriculum includes core lessons for both the classroom and the cafeteria. In the piloting of this program, we found it easier to teach the lesson in the classroom and to conduct discussion and reinforcement in the cafeteria, which is why lessons are formatted in this way. The content provided for each location is critical in fully impacting your students; however, *where* the students receive this information can be easily adapted for your school. If it is an option, you might teach the classroom content in the cafeteria, providing the students with real food and a real dining environment. However, if you are working with younger students who may be too easily distracted from eating, you might use both classroom and cafeteria content within the classroom and simply walk around the cafeteria to offer reminders during lunchtime.

We recommend instituting **"Manners on Monday"** with the teaching of the core lesson in the classroom and cafeteria, followed by the **Extending Children's Learning** lessons Tuesday through Friday. Reinforcement of the core lesson is a critical component in the success of the program, as repetition instills the qualities presented in each lesson in the hearts of your students. You can also integrate **Wilbur's Words of Wisdom** throughout the week by writing them on a board or displaying them on an interactive board in your classroom or having children recite them each morning.

How to Use this Curriculum

HOME CONNECTION

Monday is also a good day to send the **Home Connection** letter to parents or guardians to encourage their reinforcement of table manners in the home.

DISCUSSION QUESTIONS

Within **Guiding Children's Learning**, discussion questions are provided for the instructor. After encouraging the children to give their own answers, the Manners of the Heart® answers are provided in italics following each question. These are the critical points children need to fully understand how to put the instructions into practice in their daily lives.

THE PUPPET

Young children are fascinated by puppets. They are willing to set aside reality and accept what a puppet has to say. If you are willing to act a little silly, we recommend use of your Wilbur puppet as much as possible—especially in moments of stress. If a child displays unwanted aggression, puppets are a great way to diffuse the situation.

THE APRON

To smoothly transition your classroom learning from academics to table manners, put on your *Manners of the Heart®* apron. This signals your students that *Manners of the Heart®* is next.

COMMUNITY SUPPORT

Manners of the Heart® offers your school an excellent opportunity to utilize community partnerships. Many businesses in your area are concerned with the lack of social skills is the next generation and are willing to help. The lessons of *Manners of the Heart At the Table®* can be effectively taught through volunteers teaching the core lesson. In fact, for the most effective and practical use of this curriculum, we recommend involving parents, grandparents, and other community volunteers as much as possible. Teachers can then reinforce the core lesson with the **Extending Children's Learning** tips throughout the week.

How to Use this Curriculum

Check with your local discount stores about donating the paper products needed in the lessons.

We hope you will enjoy teaching table manners to your students as much as we enjoy bringing them to you!

Visit www.mannersoftheheart.org for updates, curriculum enhancements, articles and more.

> A child should always say what's true
> And speak when he is spoken to,
> And behave mannerly at the table;
> At least as far as he is able.
>
> Robert Louis Stevenson

Introduction

At the Table

Often when people think of table manners, they think of the "rules of etiquette." They think of the proper way to hold their knife or fork or the correct way to fold their napkin.

Consequently, many miss the greater value of teaching and practicing table manners.

King Louis XIV of France entertained countless guests at Versailles, his palatial palace, during his eighteenth-century reign. As much as he enjoyed his guests in the banquet hall, he was appalled by their lack of respect for his gardens. Roses were picked without permission, the meticulously kept lawn was flattened when guests left walkways to cut across the grass and flowers were trampled underfoot without regard for the imaginary boundaries.

To solve the King's dilemma, signposts, called 'etiquettes,' were placed throughout the grounds of Versailles warning visitors to "Keep off the Grass" and "Don't Walk on the Flowers." At first, visitors were not pleased with the King's imposing rules for their behavior. As the gardens flourished, however, the 'etiquettes' became welcome reminders of what not to do in order to protect the beauty of the palace grounds. Later, 'etiquettes' became tickets with instructions to social affairs within the palace walls, enabling guests to know where to stand and what to do to best enjoy the festivities.[1]

For the past century, the word 'etiquette' has come to mean all the little signs or rules that help us interact well in social situations. At Manners of the Heart®, we believe the 'rules of etiquette' are the actions that enable us to show respect for others and develop respect for ourselves.

[1] http://www.esgrace.com/didyou.html

Introduction: At The Table

Much can be learned at the dinner table about how to live life. When children learn to serve others at the table before they serve themselves, it becomes natural to put the needs of others ahead of their wants on the playground. When children learn to listen and participate in conversation at the table, they more readily listen and participate in the classroom. When children learn table manners, they're learning how to respect others and respect themselves.

Just as the purpose of the *Manners of the Heart Character Curriculum* is to teach children respectful behavior in order to support and improve a child's relationships with others, the *Manners of the Heart At the Table Etiquette Curriculum* offers an opportunity for children to learn respect and connect with others during mealtime.

To help engage your children in the process, we have created a series of stories based in Merryville, a picturesque little town between the mountains and the sea. Merryville is filled with folks and furry friends who want to help kids become all they are meant to be. The central character of Manners of the Heart, Wilbur, the wise old owl, loves children and enjoys answering their questions and sharing his wisdom about life and living. He lives in the only happle tree in the world at the foot of Merryville Mountain.

In "Wilbur's Picnic" children meet Wilbur's friends and Tommy Tripper when Tommy hears the critters' laughter from underneath the happle tree and stops to investigate.

Read "Wilbur's Picnic" (found at the end of the introduction) to your students before beginning the lessons to cultivate enthusiasm and to encourage participation in learning table etiquette.

Introduction: At The Table

WILBUR'S PICNIC

It was a beautiful day in Merryville, the little town nestled between the mountains and the sea. Tommy Tripper was on his bicycle speeding down the hill from his house just like he did everyday.

When he saw the giant tree in front of him, he remembered his first encounter with the tree that was as big around as a merry-go-round and a hundred shades of green. A few months ago, he had crashed into the big red mailbox underneath the tree and as he lay there, someone had called out, "Whooooo goes there?" It turned out to be Wilbur, the wise old owl, who lived in the tree. The only happle tree in the world. (Happles are a special fruit that are shaped like hearts and sweet as apples.)

Wise Ol' Wilbur's eyebrows reminded Tommy of the handlebars on his bike. His eyes were as black as pieces of coal. His bright yellow beak stood so far out from his face that Tommy wondered how the owl kept from falling over when he talked.

Tommy slid to a stop by the happle tree when he heard the laughter of the Merryville critters sitting at Wilbur's picnic table.

The first critters he saw at the table were Peter and Penelope, the funniest brother and sister raccoons he knew. (Penelope thinks more of herself than she ought. Peter can get in trouble sometimes, but he always means well.)

Seated across from Peter and Penelope, were Buddy and Bully, the twin bulldogs. (They look just alike except for the heart mark on Buddy's chest. You can always tell them apart by the way they act. Buddy's everybody's best friend, but it's hard for Bully to make friends because of the way he treats other people.)

Sitting next to Buddy and Bully was Sketch the Skunk who always makes a big stink.

Buzzing overhead was BillyBeeRight. (He tries to stop kids from doing the wrong thing by buzzing in on them. He keeps a lot of kids in Merryville from making big mistakes.)

Tommy couldn't help but get off his bike to walk over and say hello to his friends. Wilbur was perched on a branch over the picnic table.

"Hey, Wilbur," shouted Tommy.

"Well, hellooooo, Tommy," answered Wilbur. "I'm just getting ready to teach the critters some table manners."

Introduction: At The Table

"My momma's always working on that with me," answered Tommy.

"You know, a lot of life lessons can be learned at the table," added Wilbur. "Would you like to join us?"

"Sure thing, Wilbur," Tommy replied as he sat down at the end of the picnic table.

Wilbur turned and said, "Let's get started."

Won't you join us, too?

Chapter 1

Table Talk

Materials and Preparation

- Bean bag or soft ball (1 or more)

NOTE—For the classroom portion of this lesson, we recommend seating students in circles. They can either be seated in one large circle or in small-group circles. When teaching second or third-graders, we recommend helping them arrange their desks in groups of five or six prior to beginning the lesson. It may be easier for younger children to sit in groups of five or six on the floor or at center tables throughout the room.

Wilbur's Words of Wisdom

Table time is time to talk!

Guiding Children's Learning in the Classroom

Introduce the lesson by showing students the bean bag or ball. Explain that each student will have the opportunity to share one sentence about their day when they are given the bean bag or ball. Remind those listening not to speak when a classmate is holding the bag/ball. To begin, share one piece of information about your day and toss the bag/ball to a student. Let that student share and then toss the ball to another student (and so on until each student has had a turn). (Optional—if students are seated in groups, make sure to have one bean bag or ball per group and help them do the activity among themselves.)

Continue with a discussion, using the following questions and comments:

- Was it fun to hear about your classmates' days?
- Was it fun to share about your own day?
- What did you learn about those with whom you are sitting?
- What did others learn about you?
- Mealtime is an opportunity to spend time or 'connect' with other people by participating in conversation.

Attributes
Participation, Respectfulness

Skills and Objectives:

Children are learning ways to support their relationships with others through respectful behavior at the table. In this lesson, children will learn ways to connect with others during mealtime. Children will learn to participate by the following:
- Listening to the stories of others
- Sharing their own stories
- Being engaged with those around them

Chapter 1: Table Talk

The activity you just did is an activity some kids do with their families during dinner, only without the bean bag/ball. If you don't do this activity with your family, you could be the one to start it! Simply ask each of your brothers or sisters and your parents to share something about their day as you eat a meal together.

Do you think it is good for family members to share about their day? Why?
- *Yes, sharing about our days helps everyone understand each other better.*
- *Yes, my family will like to know why I am in a good or a bad mood after school.*

> **Definitions:**
>
> **PARTICIPATION**
> Choosing to be fully involved in the task or project at hand
>
> **RESPECTFULNESS**
> Treating others with dignity

What do you think you should do if someone asks you a question during your meal? Why?
- *Answer the question because they are trying to understand what I think or feel.*
- *Answer the question, even when I'm feeling bad, because ignoring them would make them feel bad, too.*

Using good manners at the table involves putting everything else aside for friends and family members. What sorts of electronics might get in the way of your paying attention to the people with whom you are eating?
- *The television*
- *Video games*
- *iPods*
- *The telephone*

Sometimes, adults will talk about things you may not understand or may not be able to talk about. When that happens, what can you do?
- *Quietly eat my food while letting the adults finish their conversation.*
- *If there is a break in the conversation, share something I want to talk about, making sure not to interrupt someone else.*

Conclude the classroom portion of the lesson by reminding students that mealtime is a good time to talk to the people you are with. However, it's important to remember the following:

- To participate in the conversation without talking too much
- To answer questions politely and also to think of questions to ask others
- Not to talk with your mouth full
- Not to talk about anything gross, but to practice respectful 'table talk'
- To practice eye contact by looking down to take a bite and then looking up again

You will be learning a lot more about practicing good table manners in the coming weeks! During lunch, let's practice what we have learned so far.

Chapter 1: Table Talk

Guiding Children's Learning in the Cafeteria

During lunch today or later in the week, use the following comments and questions to guide each table in a discussion:
What did you learn today/this week about eating with others?
- *Mealtime is a good time to talk with others about my day.*
- *You can't participate in the meal with others when you are watching television, playing a game, or listening to music.*

Can you think of any good reasons to sit down with others for your meal?
- *It is a lot more fun than eating alone!*
- *When you talk about your day and listen to others share about their day, it helps you understand each other.*

Sharing mealtime with others gives you the opportunity to (share the following points):
- Practice the manners you are learning through *Manners of the Heart*.
- Spend time with your family and friends.
- Hear about each person's day and feel like you were a part of it.
- Share about your own day, whether it was good or bad.

As you make your rounds, remind students of the following:
- Participate in the conversation, but don't talk too much. (If needed, gently remind students to allow their classmates to speak while they listen.)
- Answer questions politely and think of questions to ask others. (If needed, help students come up with questions to ask their classmates while eating.)
- Don't talk with your mouth full! (Teach students how to ask and answer questions in between bites.)
- Don't talk about anything gross, but practice respectful 'table talk.'
- Practice eye contact while you are eating. (Teach them how to look down to take a bite and then look up again.)

EXTENDING CHILDREN'S LEARNING

1. Allow children to express their favorite family meals using blank paper, coloring or writing utensils and the following age-appropriate activities:

    - K-1—Have students draw a picture of their favorite holiday meal. Have them explain to fellow classmates what makes this holiday meal special. Make sure students practice their listening skills while classmates discuss their drawings.

    - 2-5—Have students write a story describing their favorite holiday meal. Give them the opportunity to share their story and politely listen to the story of other classmates.

Chapter 1: Table Talk

2. Mealtime has always been an opportunity to tell and hear stories. In fact, many families from around the world use mealtime to share stories. Help students better understand this idea by bringing a visitor (e.g., the principal, music or art teacher, parent, etc.) to share or read a story while students eat their lunch or snack. Have students practice their listening skills by quietly eating and listening to the story. At the end, allow them to ask questions.

3. Ask students to share aspects of their supper tradition with the class or with a table during lunch. Do they have a seated dinner with their whole family? Does their family prefer laid-back dinners in front of the television? Are they eating on-the-run, or in between sports practices or music lessons? Do their parents work late and have to miss out on dinner with them? Ask students to share how they most enjoy spending their dinnertime (e.g., watching television, eating with their family in a quiet environment, eating in a restaurant, etc.). If appropriate, encourage students to start a new tradition with their family by organizing 'family night' for one dinner each week. Students can talk with their parents or guardians about this idea and offer to help with the planning, preparing and post-dinner cleaning.

4. Culture Tip—Lead a discussion on how different cultures participate in the family meal. For example, share the following culture tip with students:

    People in some cultures prefer to eat silently. If you are a guest in someone's home, make sure to wait until you are asked a question before speaking. This will help you know what the mealtime tradition is for that family.

5. Choose one lunch this week to have students pretend they are eating with adults in a dining environment. Ask students to show you what they have learned about being respectful and considerate toward others through the ways they eat and talk during their meal. Remind them to practice appropriate, respectful conversation with their peers. Encourage them by sharing that they will learn many helpful ways to respect others during mealtime through table manners lessons in the folowing weeks.*

*NOTE - This activity will be repeated throughout the table manners lessons, providing you and other adults with the opportunity to witness what the children are learning. We reccommend choosing one lunch each week for children to practice their dining skills. You can also plan a "Fine Dining Day" by inviting parents, grandparents and guests to the school for a meal that the children help with the preparation and clean up.

Chapter 1: Table Talk

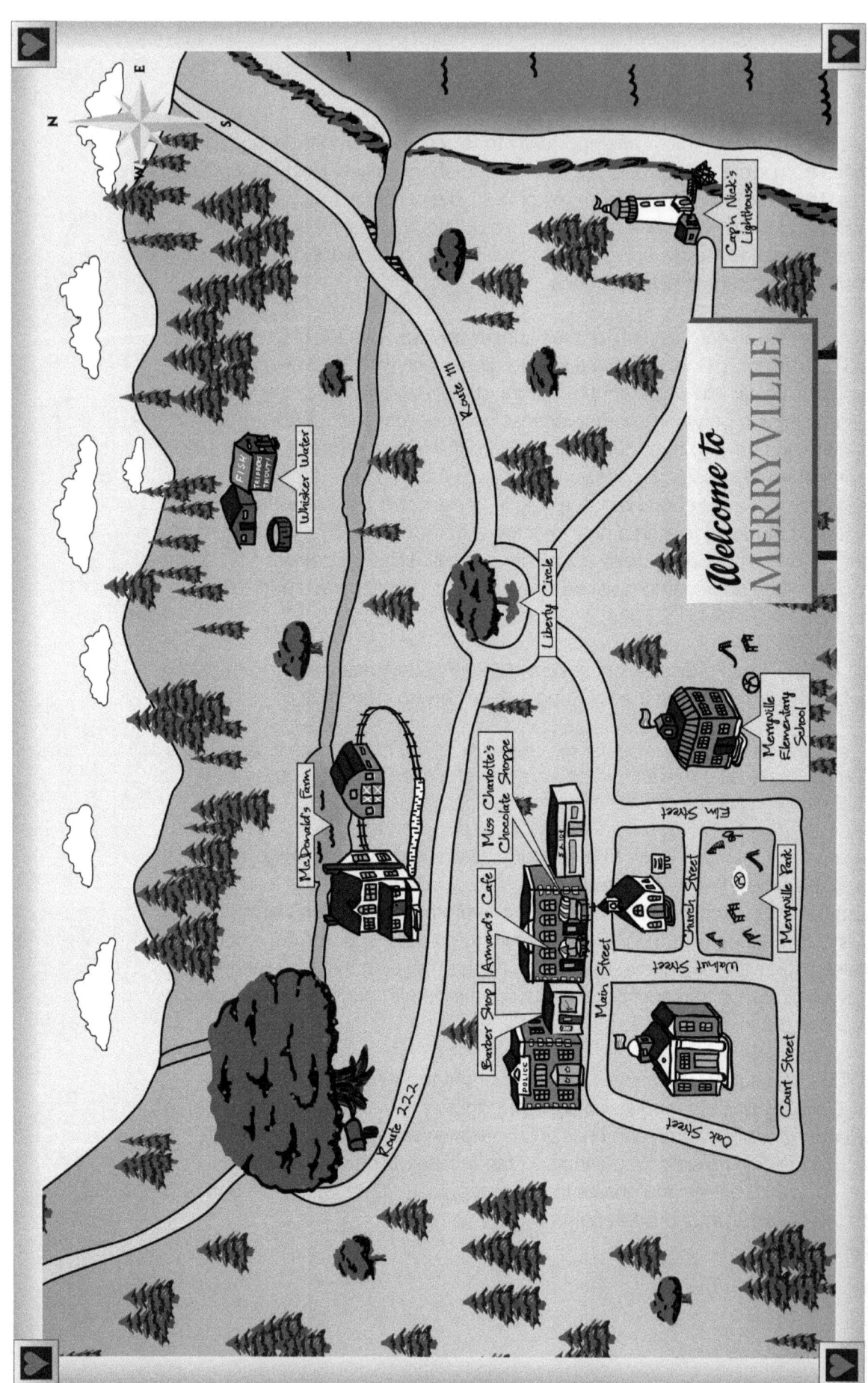

Chapter 1: Table Talk

Home Connection

Dear Parent/Guardian,

This week, students are beginning to learn the importance of table manners. These lessons really hit home because table manners (and so much more!) are best learned at the family table. Studies have found that mealtime is a more powerful influence on children than time spent in school, studying, church, playing sports or art activities. It has been found that kids who eat with their families benefit in these ways:

- They make better grades in school
- They have a more positive attitude about their future
- They are less likely to get involved with negative behaviors like drinking alcohol, taking drugs or smoking

We know it is difficult to find time to eat together as a family, but nothing can shape a child's life the way sitting around the family table can!

Making mealtime family time again will give your children something they cannot receive anywhere else—the security of a close-knit family. And while you're there, you can teach table manners and other life lessons they'll use for the rest of their lives! If mealtime in your home is less important than you want it to be, here are a few simple ideas to build family connectedness at the table:

- If you rarely sit down together, begin with just one evening a week.
- Simple, easy meals are great. You don't have to spend two hours in the kitchen!
- Prioritize your meals as family time by 'unplugging'—no television, cell phones, iPods, or video games.
- Let your children take turns choosing the menu and helping with the preparation and cleanup.
- Get out that old crockpot! Some of the most delicious and easiest meals cook all day while you're at work.
- It's okay to pick up take-out on the way home; just serve it at the dinner table.
- Family meals are for enjoyment. Save the difficult conversations for later. Refrain from scolding or arguing at the table.
- Light a candle or put flowers on the table; anything to make it special!
- If some family members have activities until late in the day, give the kids a snack after school and wait to eat dinner when everyone is home at the same time.

~ From Our Hearts To Yours

Chapter 2

Flatware Goes Somewhere

Materials and Preparation

- Copies of "Place-Setting Map" (1/student)
- Plastic forks (1/student)
- Plastic knives (1/student)
- Plastic spoons (1/student)
- Paper dinner plates (1/student)
- Paper bread/salad plates (1/student)
- Paper napkins (1/student)
- Plastic cups (1/student)

NOTE—We suggest using brightly-colored plastic and paper products for this activity as the simple, fun colors help kids become more engaged in the lesson!

Wilbur's Words of Wisdom

You can be helpful
And show you're able,
To take your time
And set the table!

Guiding Children's Learning in the Classroom

Begin the lesson by distributing the place-setting materials. Open with a brief discussion, using the following questions and comments:

- Have you been asked to set the table?

- If so, when was the last time you set the table for your family's dinner?

- Today, you are going to learn the right way to set the table. Some of you may already know this and if so, you can help your classmates!

Attributes
Appreciation, Helpfulness, Orderliness

Skills and Objectives:

Knowing how to set the table is a valuable life lesson. Setting or 'dressing' the table teaches children *appreciation* for their meal and for the person providing it. Children learn *orderliness* with the understanding that "everything has its place and everything in its place." Setting the table also provides children with the opportunity to be *helpful* by contributing to the meal. In this lesson, children will learn the following:

- The placement of utensils, plates and cups
- That 'dressing' the table for everyday meals makes the dinner table a special place to gather with family and friends

Chapter 2: Flatware Goes Somewhere

Have students use their own paper and plastic plates, cups and utensils to set their place as best they can without instruction.

Go around the room to see how everyone did on their first try. Then teach them the right way to set their place by giving them the place-setting map and using the following comments and questions. (NOTE—depending on the age of students and the allotted time for this lesson, you may want to focus only on the basics, such as the general area to place your utensils, napkin and cup.)

How many letters are in the word LEFT?
- *Four!*

And how many letters are there in the word RIGHT?
- *Five!*

> **Definitions:**
>
> **APPRECIATION**
> Recognizing and acknowledging value in people, places, and things
>
> **HELPFULNESS**
> Looking for ways to ease the burdens others carry
>
> **ORDERLINESS**
> Keeping the space around me neat and tidy

- The number of letters helps us know on which side of the plate to place our fork, knife, spoon and glass! Let's figure out where these belong:

    F-O-R-K   This has four letters like the word LEFT, so it goes on the left side of our plate!
    K-N-I-F-E   This has five letters like the word RIGHT, so it goes on the right side of our plate!
    S-P-O-O-N   This has five letters like the word RIGHT, so it goes on the right side of our plate!
    G-L-A-S-S   This has five letters like the word RIGHT, so it goes on the right side of our plate!

Since many of you are probably right-handed and scoop food on your fork with your right hand, why do you think your *fork* is placed on your *left* and your *knife* is placed on your *right*? (Help with the following by demonstrating.)
- *It makes them easier to pick up when I need to cut my food, with the knife in my right hand and the fork in my left hand.*

Where do you think the napkin should go? (Help with the following by demonstrating.)
- *On my left, next to my fork, not underneath it*
- *On the center of my plate*

The knife blade should be facing your plate and the spoon should be to the right of your knife. Why do you think the knife blade should face the plate instead of facing the spoon? (Help with the following by demonstrating.)
- *It is easier to cut my food because the blade will be pointing down.*
- *It is not nice to have my sharp knife blade facing my neighbor.*

We already know your glass or cup goes on the right side of your plate, but who can

Chapter 2: Flatware Goes Somewhere

show me where on the right side it should go? (Be silly with this! Ask if it should go at the bottom of the knife and fork, rested on top of the knife, etc.)
- *At the top of my knife*

Who knows the right place for your salad plate? Show me.
- *To the left of my fork if it is on the table the same time as my dinner plate*
- *Right in front of me if my dinner plate is not on the table*

Now pretend your salad plate is your bread plate. Where does this go?
- *On the left side of my dinner plate, above my fork and across from my glass*

Close by having students show you their place settings.

A Note on Gender:

It is important that both girls and boys are taught the importance of setting the table. While it is often not as important to boys whether they have a nice environment, it is important that boys learn to appreciate a nice environment for meals. This will give them a greater appreciation for a future spouse's efforts at meal preparation—rather than wanting to watch television during dinner, they will be accustomed to enjoying the family table.

Guiding Children's Learning in the Cafeteria

During lunch today or later in the week, use the following comments and questions to guide each table in a discussion:

Many of you probably know that you are supposed to dress nicely when you are going somewhere nice. Why do you think this is true?
- *Getting dressed up for a nice occasion helps us and others remember the specialness of where we are and what we are doing.*
- Just like you get dressed up when you go somewhere nice, the table should be dressed up when you are having a meal.

Why else do you think it is important to set the table for meals? Help them with the following points:
- *'Dressing' or 'setting' the table shows the person who spent time preparing your meal that you appreciate their hard work.*
- *When the table is set, it helps everyone in the family know that mealtime is a special time.*
- *Meals are more enjoyable for everyone when the table environment is pleasant.*
- *It is easier for everyone to enjoy their meal when they have everything they need already in place on the table (no one will need to get up for forks, knives or cups).*
- *"Everything has its place and everything in its place!"* (Ask the students to repeat this with you. The idea is that there is an assigned order to everything that goes on the table.)
- *When we know how to set the table, we will also know where to find everything when we eat in a restaurant or in someone's home.*

If time allows, let children share some of the negatives of setting the table (e.g., it takes time) and then discuss how the positive aspects of setting the table outweigh the negative aspects.

Chapter 2: Flatware Goes Somewhere

Conclude your discussion by having students correctly arrange their place setting before they enjoy their meal.

EXTENDING
CHILDREN'S LEARNING

1. Use the following age-appropriate activities with the table-setting activity sheet:

   - K-1—Have students color the table setting. Hang them in your room or have students take them home to hang on their refrigerators.

   - 2-5—Have students color the setting materials, then cut them out to practice setting the place on their own. They can also take these cut-out pieces home to show family members what they have learned about setting the table.

2. Teach students a special napkin fold. Use paper or linen napkins and the "Peter's Hat" activity sheet to make a napkin fold that is fun for both boys and girls!

3. Culture Tip—Lead a discussion on how setting the table might look a little different in other cultures. Here are some examples:

   - The French place the fork with the "tines" pointing down while those in America and England place the "tines" pointing up (demonstrate this for students). This is the same with the spoon!
   - In Asian restaurants or homes, you may be served chopsticks instead of your regular fork, spoon, and knife. (If time allows, have some fun by giving each student a set of chopsticks to try eating their lunch.)
   - In some nice dining establishments in Europe, you will not receive a bread plate but will be expected to eat your bread right off the table!

4. Use the paper and plastic place-setting materials for your "Fine Dining" day. Have students pretend they are eating their lunch at a friend's house. Ask students to show you what they have learned about setting the table prior to beginning their meal. (If students have made the placemat and/or practiced their napkin fold from the other activities in **Extending Children's Learning**, put these to use as well!). Remind students to practice appropriate, respectful conversation while eating as learned in the previous lesson.

Chapter 2: Flatware Goes Somewhere

Home Connection

Dear Parent/Guardian,

This week, students are learning how to set the table. They are learning the following:

- The placement of eating utensils, plates and cups
- That 'dressing' the table for even everyday meals makes the dinner table a special place to gather with family and friends

While it may be considered "a thing of the past," learning how to set the table is a valuable life lesson. Setting or 'dressing' the table teaches children *appreciation* for their meal and for the person who prepared it. Children learn *orderliness* with the understanding that "everything has its place and everything in its place." Setting the table also provides children with the opportunity to be *helpful* by contributing to the meal.

Ask your child to show you what he or she learned by setting the table for your next family dinner. Here are some basic table-setting rules your child is learning at school:

- There are four letters in the word LEFT and five letters in the word RIGHT. This is how children (and adults!) can remember where to place utensils and glasses. The fork (which has four letters) goes on your left and the knife, spoon, and glass (which all have five) letters go on your right.
- The fork is placed on your left and the knife is placed on your right because they are easier to pick up when you need to cut your food.
- The napkin is placed on your left, next to the fork, or on the center of your plate.
- The knife is placed to the right of your plate and the spoon is placed to the right of the knife.
- The blade of the knife should face your plate because it is easier to cut your food (the blade is already pointing down when you pick it up) and it is impolite to have the sharp blade facing your neighbor.
- The cup is placed at the top of the knife.
- The bread plate is placed to the LEFT side of the dinner plate, above the fork and across from the cup.

Encourage your child to take charge of setting the table for family meals (even kindergartners can put the napkins and utensils in the right place). You can give your child the correct number of utensils, plates, napkins and cups, and then let him or her do the work from there! You will be helping your child feel an important sense of contribution to your family's meal.

~ From Our Hearts To Yours

Chapter 2: Flatware Goes Somewhere

Peter's Hat

This is a basic napkin fold, also known as the "Bishop's Hat." Paper or cloth napkins can be used.

A few of your students will catch on to this activity quickly while others will not. This gives the perfect opportunity for your students to experience the great joy of helping others learn a skill they have mastered. As children finish making "Peter's Hat," ask them to turn to help a fellow student who may be struggling.

Using the diagram to help you follow these steps:

1. Lay the napkin open and flat in front of you.
2. Fold the napkin in half with the open side towards you.
3. Fold corners A to B and C to D, bringing opposite corners to the center.
4. Flip the napkin over and orient it so the folded edge runs parallel to the table edge.
5. Fold the bottom half of the napkin up and away from you, laying it so the folded edges run on top of one another. Reach underneath the napkin and pull out the flap on the right, making two points on the napkin as seen in the picture.
6. Gently roll the left half of the left triangle over and tuck its end underneath the right triangle.
7. Turn the napkin around and repeat step five.
8. Open up the hat by gently pulling the bottom edges apart so that it becomes circular.

There you have it: "Peter's Hat!"

*Note: You will find a tutorial video of how to fold "Peter's Hat" on our website.

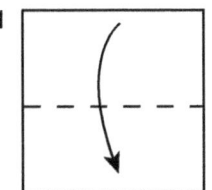
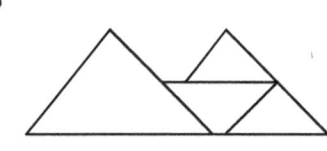

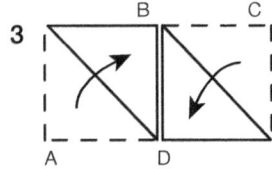

Chapter 2: Flatware Goes Somewhere

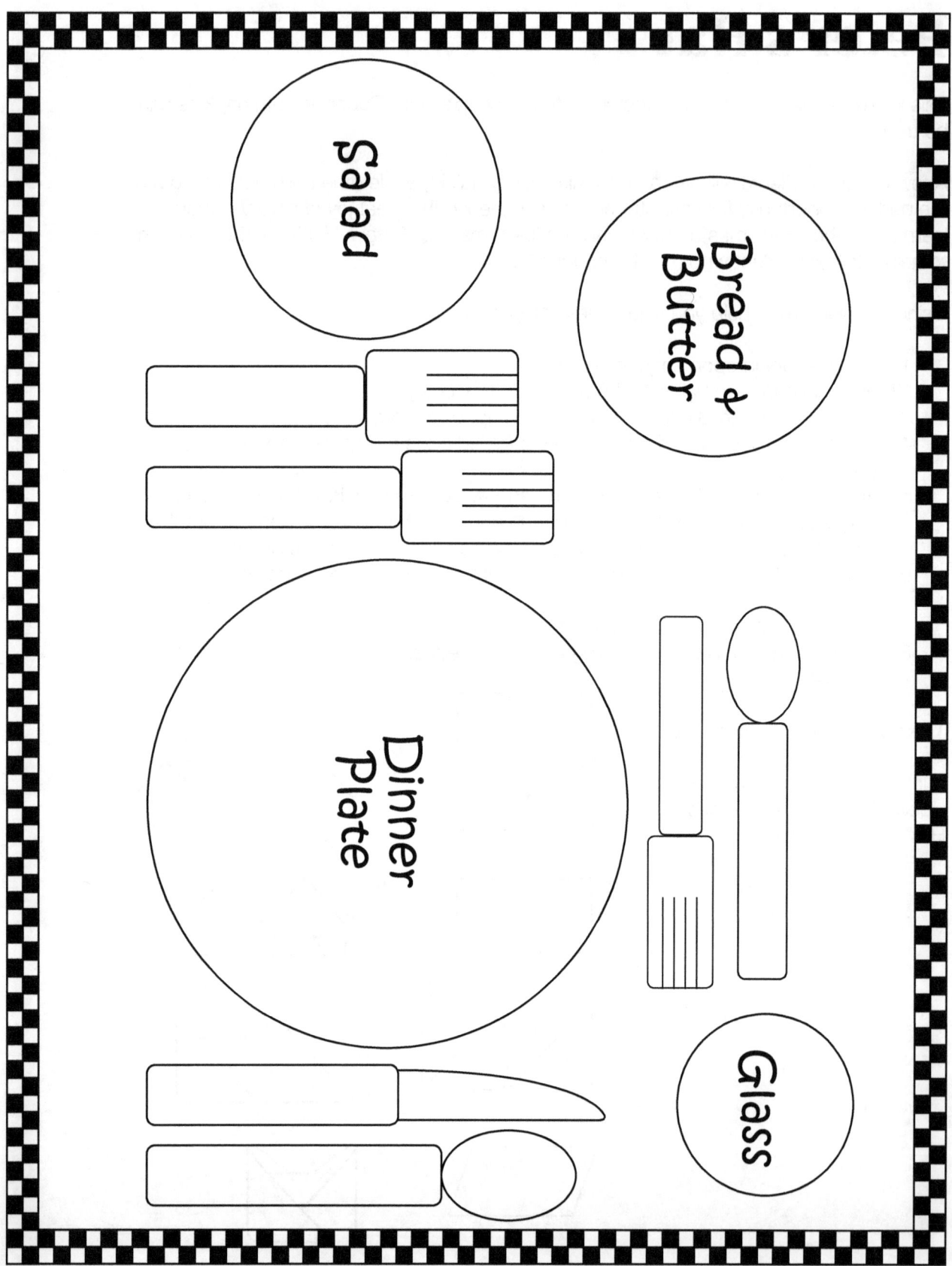

Chapter 3

Come One, Come All

Materials and Preparation

- Brightly colored napkins (1/student)

Wilbur's Words of Wisdom

Please wait and be polite
Before you take a bite.
You'll bring such great delight
Because you've done it right.

Guiding Children's Learning in the Classroom

To begin, teach students six steps to getting ready for their meal, using the tune, "The Farmer in the Dell":

> Come fast when you are called;
> Come fast when you are called.
>   Mealtime is fun for all.
> Come fast when you are called.
>
> First, wash and dry your hands;
> First, wash and dry your hands.
>   Mealtime is fun for all.
> First, wash and dry your hands.
>
> Place napkin in your lap;
> Place napkin in your lap.
>   Mealtime is fun for all.
> Place napkin in your lap.
>
> Sit straight—don't slouch—and smile;
> Sit straight—don't slouch—and smile.
>   Mealtime is fun for all.
> Sit straight—don't slouch—and smile.
>
> Be thankful for your food;
> Be thankful for your food.
>   Mealtime is fun for all.
> Be thankful for your food.

Attributes
Gratitude, Politeness

Skills and Objectives:
Before starting the meal, there are some important steps children must learn in order to exercise their politeness and gratefulness to others at the table. In this lesson, students will learn the following:
- To come when they are called
- To wash and dry their hands
- To place their napkin in their laps
- To maintain a pleasant posture and expression
- To pause with gratitude for the meal
- To wait for adults to take the first bite

> Adults should eat first bite;
> Adults should eat first bite.
>   Mealtime is fun for all.
> Adults should eat first bite!

Chapter 3: Come One, Come All

Sing the song several times until your students can remember the words. Then, tell students you are going to talk a little more about why these steps are important. Use the following comments and questions:

Why do you think it is important to come quickly when you are called?
- *Coming right away shows your parent or teacher that you are a good listener and that you can be trusted.*
- *Coming right away shows politeness for the person who prepared the food and for everyone else who will be eating it. It is not nice to have others waiting on you when they are hungry—especially if the food is getting cold!*

Why do you think it is important to wash and dry your hands?
- *Germs! You have been touching germs all day, and you may not even know it. These germs can make you or others sick if you don't wash them off before eating your food.*
- *If your hands look dirty, it is harder for others to enjoy their food.*
- *It is not only important to wash your hands with water and soap, but also to dry them off so you can be completely ready for the meal. If you don't dry your hands, they will be slippery, and you might accidentally drop your plate.*
- *If you are with people who hold hands while they say a prayer, it is not nice to have a dirty or wet hand for them to hold.*

Why do you think it is important to sit straight and smile at the table?
- *Everyone at the table will be more able to enjoy their meal when you behave politely by sitting straight and smiling.*
- *When you slouch, it is hard for your food to make its way to your belly.*
- *Sitting straight and smiling shows others you are thankful for being part of the meal.*

Act out several impolite body postures and facial expressions. Ask your students whether or not these gestures are pleasant to see. (For example, have them tell you if they would like to eat a meal with someone who was frowning and slouching in the chair with their arms crossed.)

Conclude the classroom portion of the lesson by having students recite "Mealtime is Fun for All" one final time. Let students know they will be talking about the other steps involved in getting ready for the meal while they eat their lunch.

Guiding Children's Learning in the Cafeteria

During lunch today or later in the week, distribute a fun-colored napkin to students as they pick up their meals and take their seats in the cafeteria. Begin by showing students how to place their napkin in their lap. Then, use the following questions and comments to guide each table in a discussion while students eat their meal:

Chapter 3: Come One, Come All

Why do you think it's important to place your napkin in your lap?
- *Food might fall on your lap while you are eating. It is better for food to fall on your napkin than on your clothes!*
- *It is easier to wipe your mouth or your fingers when the napkin is already in your lap.*
- *People don't want to look at your dirty napkin if it is sitting on the table!*

I want to see you setting a good example for the rest of the school by placing your napkin in your lap the first thing when you sit down for lunch!

> **Definitions:**
>
> **GRATITUDE**
> Appreciating what you have
>
> **POLITENESS**
> Using kind words and actions in all situations

Now, when you are seated at the table and have placed your napkin in your lap, is it time to start eating? (No!)

First, before you start eating, you need to show others that you are thankful for your food. What are some ways to show others your thankfulness for your food?
- *Thank the person who prepared it or who is serving your food by saying, "Thank you for the food" or "This looks really good!"*
- *If you are a guest in someone's home, say, "Thank you for having me. This looks great!"*
- *Participate in grace or a blessing.*

Many families begin their meal with a blessing or grace. Even if this is not what your family usually does, it is important that you wait to start eating in someone else's home in case they begin with a blessing.

If the people you are with say grace, be respectful while it is said. How can you show respect during the blessing?
- *Stay silent and bow your head.*
- *Close your eyes or keep them on your lap.*
- *Fold your hands, or if everyone else holds hands, gently hold your neighbor's hand without fidgeting.*

What is the final step to remember before you start eating your food? (Adults should eat first bite.) Why should adults eat the first bite of food?

- *Waiting for adults to take the first bite lets you know when it is okay to start eating. (It is important to wait until you know it is okay to begin eating, especially when you are in another person's home with different mealtime traditions.)*
- *Since you were probably not the person who bought or cooked the food, it is polite to wait until the person who did do these things begins to eat. This shows the person who prepared the food that you are thankful.*
- *Even when adults are not around, you can show respect for those around you by waiting to eat until everyone at your table is seated.*

Conclude by thanking students for their participation in today's lesson and encouraging them to practice their six steps before every meal this week.

Chapter 3: Come One, Come All

EXTENDING
CHILDREN'S LEARNING

1. Using the "Thankful Poems" activity sheet, have students color and cut out their poems. Give each student a sticker magnet so they can put the poems on their refrigerator at home.

2. Teach students the correct way to place a napkin in their lap—not by folding it in half, but by folding a third of the napkin down. Only this top folded piece should be used to wipe the mouth. When you fold the napkin by a third, there is plenty of napkin underneath the folded piece to keep food that has been wiped from getting on your clothes.

3. Each day during the week, have students sing "Mealtime is Fun for All" before leaving the classroom at lunchtime or as they enter the cafeteria. Have them sing the song for their cafeteria or lunch ladies, or any parent volunteers who help out during lunch. These adults can help keep students accountable to their six steps to getting ready for the meal.

4. On your "Fine Dining" day, have students pretend they are eating lunch with adults. Ask students to tell you what they have learned about being polite and grateful during mealtime. Have them act out each of the six steps in getting ready for the meal. Afterwards, ask them to tell you why these steps are important to practice in a restaurant. As a review from the last two lessons, remind students to practice considerate conversation and to set their place before eating.

Chapter 3: Come One, Come All

Home Connection

Dear Parent/Guardian,

This week, your child is learning six important steps to getting ready for a meal. You can reinforce what your child is learning at school and also have some fun by using "Mealtime is Fun for All" (use the tune of "The Farmer in the Dell"). Ask your child to recite the song and teach it to the rest of your family. If you don't mind acting a little goofy, sing it along with your child while he or she is getting ready for the meal throughout the week.

Mealtime is Fun for All

Come fast when you are called;
Come fast when you are called.
　Mealtime is fun for all.
Come fast when you are called.

First, wash and dry your hands;
First, wash and dry your hands.
　Mealtime is fun for all.
First, wash and dry your hands.

Place napkin in your lap;
Place napkin in your lap.
　Mealtime is fun for all.
Place napkin in your lap.

Sit straight—don't slouch—and smile;
Sit straight—don't slouch—and smile.
　Mealtime is fun for all.
Sit straight—don't slouch—and smile.

Be thankful for your food;
Be thankful for your food.
　Mealtime is fun for all.
Be thankful for your food.

Adults should eat first bite;
Adults should eat first bite.
　Mealtime is fun for all.
Adults should eat first bite.

~ From Our Hearts To Yours

Chapter 3: Come One, Come All

Thankful Poems

We are thankful for happy hearts,
For rain and sunny weather.
We are thankful for this our food
And that we are together.

Adapted from a poem by
Emille Fendall Johnson

We are thankful for this food,
For rest and home and all things good
For wind and rain and sun above.
But, most of all, for those we love.

Adapted from a poem by
Mary Leona Frost

For every cup and plateful,
We are truly grateful.

Adapted from a poem by
A.S.T. Fisher

Chapter 3: Come One, Come All

Mealtime is Fun for All

Come fast when you are called;
Come fast when you are called.
   Mealtime is fun for all.
Come fast when you are called.

First, wash and dry your hands;
First, wash and dry your hands.
   Mealtime is fun for all.
First, wash and dry your hands.

   Place napkin in your lap;
   Place napkin in your lap.
   Mealtime is fun for all.
   Place napkin in your lap.

Sit straight—don't slouch—and smile;
Sit straight—don't slouch—and smile.
   Mealtime is fun for all.
Sit straight—don't slouch—and smile.

   Be thankful for your food;
   Be thankful for your food.
   Mealtime is fun for all.
   Be thankful for your food.

   Adults should eat first bite;
   Adults should eat first bite.
   Mealtime is fun for all.
   Adults should eat first bite.

Chapter 4

Mess Hall Manners

Materials and Preparation

- Wise Ol' Wilbur puppet
- Plate (1 total)
- Fork (1 total)
- Napkin (1 total)

NOTE—This lesson will get silly! Manners of the Heart® has found that when adults are willing to be silly and make themselves messy for children, the laughter opens their hearts to receive the lesson you're trying to teach. Through the silliness, children are more likely to hear what is said and, therefore, more likely to internalize the objectives.

NOTE—We recommend teaching this lesson with a partner with one of you acting as "Miss Mess" and one of you acting as Wilbur.

Wilbur's Words of Wisdom

Miss Mess is finally starting to see... Eating with others involves courtesy!

Guiding Children's Learning in the Classroom

In this lesson, *you'll* be the one who needs to learn good table manners! Place your plate, fork and napkin in front of you, as if you were sitting at the table for a meal. Then, introduce the students to "Miss Mess."

Following the script below, act out each inappropriate table behavior. After each behavior, ask the students to tell you if your actions were respectful or not, and then have students tell or show you the right way to behave. Use Wilbur to further explain courteous and considerate table behavior. (**NOTE**—If time does not permit that you use each of the following, choose the examples that your students are most in need of learning.)

YOU—(Slouch with your elbows on the table and look bored.)

Wilbur—"While you are at the table, you need to sit straight with your feet flat on the floor

Attributes
Consideration, Courtesy

Skills and Objectives:

If courteous behavior at the table is taught and reinforced when children are young, it becomes second nature as they grow. Meals become a time to enjoy the company of others, rather than just a time to 'stuff your face'! In this lesson, children will learn the following:
- Discourteous or inappropriate table behavior
- Courteous or appropriate table behavior
- Why it is important to practice courteous table behavior

Chapter 4: Mess Hall Manners

in front of you. It is hard for others to enjoy their meal with you if it looks like you would rather be doing something else instead of eating with them! Slouching at mealtime also makes it harder for the food to go down."

YOU—(Move anxiously all around.)

Wilbur—"No need to be moving around! Show others you can be trusted to sit still and keep your hands and feet to yourself. It is hard for others to enjoy their meal when you are moving around because it makes them feel uncomfortable or anxious. The best place for your hands is in your lap when they are not working to put food or drink into your mouth."

YOU—(Lean back in your chair.)

Wilbur—"Leaning back in your chair is pretty disrespectful to the person who paid for the chair. If you lean back in your chair, the legs could snap or the chair could fall, and you would end up on the floor! Even if you don't get hurt and the chair doesn't get scratched, the others you are eating with can't enjoy their meal if you are moving around and falling on the floor."

YOU—(Complain obnoxiously about the food. For example, say "This is gross!" or "I'm not going to eat this!")

Wilbur—"Complaining about the food is very hurtful to the person who prepared it.

Even if the person who made your food can't hear you, such as the cafeteria lady or the chef at a restaurant, complaining makes others sitting around you feel uncomfortable. No one likes to be around someone who always complains!

All throughout your life, you will be introduced to new foods that you need to try. We call it a 'courtesy bite.' If you don't like it after the first bite, you don't have to eat anymore, but don't make a face and don't complain about the food.

> **Definitions:**
>
> **CONSIDERATION**
> Taking into account the feelings of others before you speak or act
>
> **COURTESY**
> Gentle kindnesses shown others

It also makes it a lot more fun to eat in another person's home or in a restaurant when you like to eat a lot of different foods. If there is something you know you can't eat, just politely say 'No, thank you.'"

YOU— (Wipe your mouth with your shirt sleeve, then ask kids if this was the right thing to do. When they say "no", wipe your mouth and whole face 'ferociously' with the napkin, rather than gently blotting it.)

Wilbur—"Is it nice to look at someone who has food on their face?" (Wait for response.) "No! This can be pretty gross to the people you are eating with. You should definitely use your napkin rather than your shirt sleeve to wipe your mouth, but should you wipe your face all over with the napkin like that?" (Wait for response.) "No! Instead, you should use your napkin to gently wipe around your mouth—we call this 'blotting' your mouth."

YOU—(Wave your fork around while you are talking.)

Wilbur—"Doing this can be dangerous because you might accidentally poke somebody! Also, waving your food will cause pieces of food to fall on the table or onto a neighbor's plate. Instead, hold the food over your plate as you eat, and when you are talking or taking a drink of something, leave your food and utensils on your plate."

YOU—(Talk about something gross, such as bugs or worms.)

Wilbur—"Why is this not nice table behavior?" (Wait for response.) "It's hard to enjoy your own food when someone else is talking about something gross! Remember there is a right time and a wrong time to talk about certain things. If anything might be 'gross' to someone who is eating, don't say it!"

Conclude by using Wilbur to make the following points:

- Good table behavior is called 'courteous' behavior.
- Let's practice courteous table behavior every time we eat with other people.
- Other people will enjoy eating with you more if you are courteous when you eat!

Guiding Children's Learning in the Cafeteria

Bring Miss Mess to the cafeteria for some fun and messy instruction on courteous table manners. You will need a tray of food. Do the following role-play with each table, asking students what might be wrong following each behavior. Use Wilbur for additional teaching:

YOU—(Take a bite of food and let the food get all over your face, but don't wipe it off. Now, lick your fingers obnoxiously.)

Wilbur—"It's great that you are enjoying your food, but licking your fingers can be very unpleasant for the people around you who are trying to enjoy their food. Instead of licking your fingers, use your napkin to wipe your hands."

YOU—(Take another bite and start talking with your mouth full.)

Wilbur—"Why do you think it's wrong to talk with your mouth full?" (Wait for response.) "There are a few reasons why it's not nice to talk with your mouth full.

First, it is gross for other people around you to look at!

Second, it is easy for food to accidentally fly out of your mouth, which is also very unkind to the people eating around you.

Chapter 4: Mess Hall Manners

Third, you might choke on your food! It is best to take small bites, then chew and swallow with your mouth closed before talking."

Show students how to take small bites and chew and swallow with their mouths closed.

In making your rounds through the cafeteria, remind students to practice the courteous behavior they learned in the core lesson:

- Not slouching
- Not moving around anxiously
- Not leaning back in their chairs
- Not complaining about the food
- Not leaving food on their faces
- Not licking their fingers
- Not talking with their mouths full
- Using their napkins instead of their shirt sleeves
- Blotting instead of 'ferociously wiping' their faces
- Not waving food around
- Not talking about anything gross

Chapter 4: Mess Hall Manners

EXTENDING
CHILDREN'S LEARNING

1. Do the following age-appropriate activity sheet activities:

    - K-2—Have students draw a picture of 'bad' table behavior and a picture of 'good' table behavior, using the two columns on their activity sheet.

    - 3-5—Have students make a list of 'courteous' table behavior and a list of 'discourteous' table behavior, using the two columns on their activity sheet.

2. Later in the week, have students help you create a chart of 'courteous' and 'discourteous' table behavior on white poster board. Label the 'courteous' column with a smiling face and the 'discourteous' column with a frowning face. If these behaviors aren't mentioned by the students, make sure they are discussed and added to the chart:

• Wiping mouth with sleeve • Leaving food on face • Slurping soup • Elbows on the table • Slouching in the chair • Licking fingers • Talking with mouth full • Drinking (soup or cereal) out of a bowl	• Chewing with mouth closed • Hands in lap • Small bites • Sitting still • Straight posture • Polite conversation • Complimenting the food • Trying new foods (i.e., eating a 'courtesy bite')

    Hang the chart in the dining area as a reminder to students of courteous and discourteous table behavior. You and the students can continue to add good and bad table behavior to the list throughout the week, or for as long as the chart is posted.

3. Read *Good Table Manners for Little Monkeys* by Susie Lee Jin (Harvest House Publishers, 2009). This is a cute story that makes learning courteous table behavior fun for kids.

4. On your "Fine Dining" day, have students pretend they are eating lunch with other adults in a fine dining establishment. First, ask students to set the table for you and practice their steps in getting ready for the meal. Then, have students show you what they have learned about courteous table behavior as they eat their meal. Let kids remind each other of what is courteous and discourteous table behavior as they eat and quietly remind students who forget the courteous way to eat at the dining table. Also, remind students to practice appropriate, respectful conversation with their peers while eating.

Chapter 4: Mess Hall Manners

Home Connection

Dear Parent/Guardian,

This week, students are being engaged in a fun activity as they learn how to exercise courteous behavior at the table. We want you to have just as much fun at home with table manners as your child is having at school! This week, we're challenging you to "turn the table," so to speak, and let your child teach you a thing or two about table manners.

Using the examples below as a guide, try doing everything WRONG at the dinner table so your child can teach you everything RIGHT! Integrate your own family's rules regarding behavior at the table as much as possible while helping your child understand why it is important to practice courtesy and consideration during meals.

- Slouch with your elbows on the table (look bored).
- Move anxiously all around.
- Lean back in your chair.
- Complain obnoxiously about the food (e.g., "This is gross!" or "I'm not going to eat this!").
- Take a bite of food and let the food get all over your face, but don't wipe it off.
- Lick your fingers obnoxiously.
- Wipe your mouth with your shirt sleeve; then wipe your mouth and whole face 'ferociously' with the napkin rather than gently blotting it.
- Take another bite and start talking with your mouth full.
- Wave your food or fork around while you are talking.
- Talk about something gross (e.g., bugs).
- When someone asks you a question, ignore him or her.

Having fun yet? We know your child is having a blast and learning a lot in the process! When you're willing to be a bit foolish for the sake of your child, not only will your child enjoy the fun time, but he or she will respect you even more!

~ From Our Hearts To Yours

Chapter 4: Mess Hall Manners

Table Manners

Chapter 5

Tools of the Table

Materials and Preparation

- Plastic forks (1/student)
- Plastic knives (1/student)
- Plastic spoons (1/student)
- Paper plates (1/student)

NOTE—The cafeteria portion of this lesson is best taught when children are eating food that requires the use of utensils (e.g., pasta or chicken). If possible, plan this lesson around a cafeteria meal that will involve utensils, or better yet, have a special meal prepared for this week's lesson. Lasagna, for example, is easy and inexpensive to cook for large groups and is a great meal for teaching young children how to use plastic forks and knives.

NOTE—For younger groups of students, we recommend having a few extra teachers or volunteers to assist students with the use of their utensils in the cafeteria lesson.

Attributes
Carefulness, Self-Control

Skills and Objectives:
Properly using utensils is an opportunity for children to demonstrate their *carefulness* and *self-control*. In this lesson, children will learn the following:
- When and how to use different utensils
- How to correctly cut their food
- Ways to demonstrate carefulness and self-control while eating

Wilbur's Words of Wisdom

You're growing up!
It's not too soon
To cut your food
And use your spoon!

Guiding Children's Learning in the Classroom

Give each child their plastic utensils and paper plates to begin the lesson. As students take their utensils, give them a few basic instructions:

- Your fork, spoon and knife are called eating utensils.

- It is very important to be careful in moving these utensils, especially when setting the table or clearing your plate—this is even true for plastic forks and knives!

- Just as you don't run while carrying a pencil, you never run while carrying eating utensils.

Chapter 5: Tools of the Table

- The right way to carry your utensils is by holding them DOWN, away from your face. The reason is that you might slip or fall while you are carrying your fork or knife, and if this happens, you want to make sure they will not hurt you.

Ask students to set their place, recalling what they have already learned. Then, hold up each utensil, one at a time, and ask students to tell you what each is for:

- The FORK—Cutting soft food and for putting bites in your mouth
- The KNIFE—Cutting tougher food (e.g., meat) or buttering bread
- The SPOON—Stirring tea or for eating soup or dessert

Use the following instructions to demonstrate how to hold your fork and knife when cutting. (Have students practice with their plastic utensils, paper plates, and pretend food after each step.)

- Hold your index finger up on each hand, and say: "When cutting, hold the knife in your RIGHT hand with the index finger pointed down the knife and resting on the top of the blade. This helps you to press down when cutting." Ask your students to practice holding their knives.

- Hold the fork in your LEFT hand, and say: "The fork is used to hold the food in place while you cut back and forth with the knife." Ask your students to practice holding the food in place with their forks.

- Show your students how to hold the fork for cutting and then say: "When cutting, be careful not to wrap your hand *all* the way around the handle of your fork. Instead, place your index finger toward the bottom of your fork to keep it steady and wrap your other fingers around it. This may feel funny at first, but it will become easier the more you do it."

- "You should cut only one, or maybe two, pieces of food at a time. Eat this food before cutting more." Ask your students to practice cutting one piece.

- Show your students where to rest the knife on the dinner plate, and then say: "After you have finished cutting, lay the knife across the top right edge of your dinner plate." Ask your students to place their knives on the edge of their plates.

- Encourage your students by saying: "Cutting your own food shows others you can be careful and responsible!"

A few other reminders:

- The size of your fork is important. It tells you how big your bite should be. Your bite should not be much bigger than your fork, or it will be too big to put in your mouth without getting food on your face.

- When you are eating, keep your fork in your RIGHT hand.

Chapter 5: Tools of the Table

- You should scoop vegetables with your fork, rather than 'stabbing' them. It is okay to 'stab' lettuce, though.

- You can use your fork to cut soft foods. What are some soft foods you might cut with your fork?

    - fish
    - pasta
    - pies
    - cakes

NOTE—Most left-handed adults prefer to eat right-handed, but each child will decide for himself which is most comfortable. Allow left-handed children to experiment with holding the fork in the left hand and the knife in the right hand as they work through this lesson.

Conclude the lesson by allowing students to practice using their utensils. Assist them as needed.

> **Definitions:**
>
> **CAREFULNESS**
> Respect for your surroundings
>
> **SELF-CONTROL**
> The ability to manage yourself when no one is looking

Chapter 5: Tools of the Table

Guiding Children's Learning in the Cafeteria

During lunch today or later in the week, give students the opportunity to put their new skills to use with real food (see **Materials and Preparation**). If one or two students are doing an especially good job cutting, have them show this to the rest of their table.

Use the following questions and comments to guide each table in a discussion as they eat:

Don't wave your utensils in the air while you are talking between bites. Why do you think you should not wave your fork, knife or spoon in the air?
- *You might hurt yourself.*
- *You might hurt someone else.*
- *Food might fall onto the table or on another plate.*
- *It is gross to look at when food has touched it.*

Instead, leave your utensils on your plate in between bites. The only time you should lift your fork or spoon from your plate is when you are cutting or moving food directly into your mouth.

If you have already used your fork, spoon or knife, don't place it back on the table, but rather rest it on your plate. Why do you think you should leave your utensils on your plate instead of on the table?
- *It makes a mess on the table.*
- *It shows respect to the person who will have to clean the table.*
- *It keeps germs from spreading.*

Take your time while eating with your fork or knife. Correctly using your fork and knife takes longer, but why do you think this might be a good thing?
- *Eating slowly allows you and your family or friends to enjoy extra time with each other.*
- *Eating slowly also keeps you from eating more than your body needs.*

Don't take bites that are too big! You may be really hungry or feel that you are in a hurry, but it is important for you to take small bites. Why do you think this is important?
- *You can choke on your food.*
- *You can quickly chew and swallow your food in order to say something.*
- *It is easier for your mouth to chew.*
- *It is easier for your stomach to digest.*

Assist students who need help with their utensils while making your rounds through the cafeteria.

Chapter 5: Tools of the Table

EXTENDING
CHILDREN'S LEARNING

1. Have students make a special placemat using the following materials:

   - 17" x 22" brightly colored construction paper
   - Construction paper cut-outs of hearts (2/student), 3" squares (2/student), 1" white squares (30/student), and 1" red squares (30/student)
   - Glue or glue sticks (1/student)

   Children can glue their cut-outs onto the mat. Here is the Manners of the Heart® sample design (but children can glue their pieces anywhere):

   NOTE—Laminating the placemats will help them last longer.

   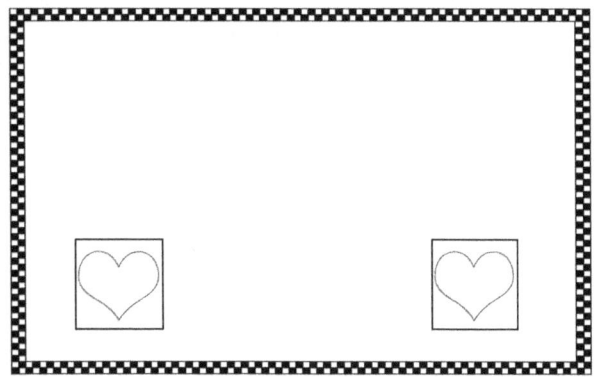

2. Challenge the students with a quiz on what they already know about table manners and help them think about some things they have yet to learn. Tell them to give you a "thumbs-up" if the statement is true and a "thumbs-down" if the statement is not true.

   - Your FORK goes on the LEFT side of your plate. (True.)
   - Your KNIFE goes on the LEFT side of your plate. (False; it goes on the RIGHT.)
   - Your SPOON goes on the RIGHT side of your plate. (True.)
   - In a nice restaurant, the salad is always served at the same time as the meal and dessert. (False. In a nice restaurant, these are typically served at different times, called *courses*. The salad or soup course is usually first, followed by the main meal, followed by dessert.)
   - When the food is served, you should wait for an adult to take the first bite of food. (True, no matter where you are eating!)
   - If you have more than one fork, it is there just for decoration. (False. They will be used for different courses of food, such as salad or dessert.)
   - In a nice restaurant, you do not need to place your napkin in your lap. (False. You should place your napkin in your lap EVERYWHERE you eat, especially in a nice restaurant!)
   - You should not eat with your elbows on the table. (True.)
   - When you are eating in a nice restaurant, you should not say anything during the meal. (False. You should participate in the conversation with others by asking and answering questions.)
   - It's okay to talk while you are chewing (False. No matter where you are eating, you should not talk while you have food in your mouth.)

Chapter 5: Tools of the Table

3. Host a competition to see who can cut the most bite-sized pieces of food within thirty seconds, using a plastic knife, plastic fork and clay shaped like a steak. Make sure they are holding their knife and fork according to the basic etiquette they have learned. Kids who are cutting their food "incorrectly" should be disqualified.

4. For your "Fine Dining" day, show students how to set the table with extra utensils (e.g., salad, dinner and dessert forks, butter knife and spoon). Have students pretend they are eating their lunch with adults. Have students practice steps in getting ready for the meal and show you what they have learned about courteous table behavior as they eat. Let students kindly remind each other of what is courteous and discourteous table behavior and quietly remind students who forget the courteous way to eat in a nice environment. Also, remind students to practice appropriate, respectful conversation with their peers while eating.

Chapter 5: Tools of the Table

Home Connection

Dear Parent/Guardian,

Properly using utensils is an opportunity for children to demonstrate their *carefulness* and *self-control*. This week, your child is learning the following:

- When and how to use different utensils
- How to correctly cut food
- Ways to demonstrate carefulness and self-control while eating

Here are some suggestions to support your child's development of carefulness and self-control through the proper use of dining utensils:

- It is tempting to prepare easy 'finger foods' for kids, rather than food that will require the use of utensils. We encourage you to prepare food that will require the use of forks, knives and spoons even when your child is young! Kids as young as preschool can learn the correct way to cut their food using a butter knife. While young kids may need help cutting more difficult foods, such as chicken or steak, elementary kids should start cutting their own food. Don't be afraid to let your child try this under your supervision.

- Prepare a nice meal and let your child set the table. Don't be afraid to give him several different utensils and teach him the correct placement of each (e.g., dessert fork or spoon at the top of the plate; salad fork on the outside of the dinner fork). You can use dinner forks and spoons as the dessert and salad utensils.

- If your family has an upcoming dinner planned in a restaurant, take the time to show your child the place setting throughout the meal. Fine restaurants will often move the utensils for you as you eat, removing your fork or knife after it is used, and bringing dessert utensils before the dessert is served. Point this out to your child and have your child tell you the correct use of each utensil that is on your table throughout the meal.

~ From Our Hearts To Yours

Chapter 6

Pass the Plate, Please

Materials and Preparation

- Paper plates (1/student)
- Slices of bread, rolls or crackers (1/student)
- Bread basket(s) (1/circle of students)
- Salt and pepper shakers (for Cafeteria learning)

NOTE—For the classroom portion of this lesson, students will need to be seated in circles. They can either be seated in one large circle or in small group circles. When teaching second or third-graders, we recommend helping them arrange their desks in groups of five or six prior to the lesson. For younger students, it may be easier having them sit in groups of five or six on the floor or at center tables throughout the room.

Wilbur's Words of Wisdom

To choose your bite,
Look with just your eyes.
Then pass to the right,
To show you're wise.

Guiding Children's Learning in the Classroom

Attributes
Awareness, Selflessness, Sharing

Skills and Objectives:

When children learn to respect the needs of others at the table, they naturally begin to demonstrate respect in other areas of life. In this lesson, children will learn the following:
- To pass food to the right
- To begin passing food that is in front of them
- To politely wait for food that is being passed
- To make a selection using their eyes and *then* their hand

To begin, distribute the plates and place a bread basket with bread, rolls or crackers inside the circle of each group of students (NOTE—intentionally position the basket in front of one child's place in each group). Instruct children to place their plate in front of them.

Use the following instructions to teach students how to pass politely and choose their food:

- Each of you is sitting in a group with your classmates. I want you to point to the person in your group whose plate is closest to the bread basket.

- This person should be able to reach for the bread basket without crossing another classmate's plate.

Chapter 6: Pass the Plate, Please

- This is how you pass food at the dinner table. The person who is closest to the food should pick it up to begin passing it. You should not lean over someone else to reach for food. Notice whose plate is closest to the food, and if this person does not realize it, politely remind him or her by saying, "_____, would you please begin passing the _____?" Practice saying this to the person in your group who is closest to the basket.

If the food has not been passed around yet, do you think it would be polite to ask for it to be passed right to you? (*No.*) What should you do instead?
- *Politely wait for the food to be passed to you.*
- *Politely ask the person closest to the food to begin passing it (but not to pass it directly to you if others to the left of you have not had any).*

The person who is in front of the bread basket can go ahead and pass it to the person on his or her RIGHT. Show me which direction is RIGHT (help them, if needed). You always pass to the person who is on your right or closest to your right hand.

Each person can take one slice/roll/cracker and then pass the basket to the person on his or her right until the first person receives it again.

When you are eating with others at the table, why do you think it is important not to take too much of the food that is being passed?
- *If you take more than your share, the food might run out before everyone has had their portion.*
- *You should not waste food by taking more than you can eat.*
- *You can always ask for more if there is food left over.*

If you do not want what is being passed, you should take a small serving to try a 'courtesy bite.' We call it a courtesy bite, because it shows respect and courtesy to the person who prepared the food. If you can't eat the food for some reason, you don't have to take any, but don't make a face. Keep passing it to the others in your group.

> **Definitions:**
>
> **AWARENESS**
> Open eyes and an open heart to the needs of others
>
> **SELFLESSNESS**
> Choosing to give of yourself with no expectation of return or consideration of loss
>
> **SHARING**
> Offering the best you have to others

When something is passed to you, choose the piece you would like with your EYES and then pick it up without touching any other pieces. Don't touch the other pieces to find the best-looking one. Why do you think it is important to touch only your own piece?
- *It shows respect for the other people eating because you are not trying to take the best for yourself.*
- *It shows respect for others because you are not giving them your germs.*
- *It shows respect for others because they are not waiting a long time for you to pick your food.*

Chapter 6: Pass the Plate, Please

When the first person who passed the basket receives it again, he/she should put it back where it was sitting in front them.

Place the bread basket(s) in front of other students to give them the opportunity to begin passing it. Remind students to politely do the following: (1) wait for the food to be passed, (2) pass to their right and (3) make a selection (or a pretend selection if the food is gone) with their eyes. Remind students to say "Thank you" when they receive the basket and to politely say, "Here is the _____ (bread, crackers, etc....)" when passing it on.

Close by teaching students **Wilbur's Words of Wisdom** to help them remember the important points about passing and selecting food.

Guiding Children's Learning in the Cafeteria

Bring salt and pepper shakers for this week's cafeteria instruction. During lunch today or later in the week, use the following comments and questions to guide each table in a discussion. Place the salt and pepper shakers on the table prior to the discussion:

Let's say that you would really like salt for your meal, but the salt shaker is not directly in front of your plate. What do you think you should do?
- *Ask the person who is closest to the salt and pepper shakers to pass it by saying, "_____, would you please pass the salt?" (Let students practice saying this to the person closest to the salt and pepper.)*

- *Here's something else that's interesting: the salt and pepper are best friends, and they always stay together. So if someone asks for the salt, you also pass the pepper!*

When the person who is closest to the salt and pepper is asked to pass it, do you think it would be polite if he or she uses the salt or pepper first before passing it on? (*No.*) Why not?
- *It is not polite because it looks like you care more about yourself than the other person who asked for it.*
- *It is not polite because the person who noticed it and asked for it has to wait longer to get it.*

What should you say when the salt and pepper are passed to you?
- *Always say "Thank you" with a smile!*

As you make your rounds, remind students of the following:

- Don't reach across your neighbor to get something on the table, but rather politely ask your neighbor to pass it.

Chapter 6: Pass the Plate, Please

- Choose your food with your eyes and touch only the piece you are taking. Do this even when you are choosing something from the cafeteria line!
- When passing food, pass it to your right.
- If someone asks for something, pass it on without helping yourself first. After the other person has had some, you can then ask to use it.

EXTENDING CHILDREN'S LEARNING

1. Gather your students into a circle. Give every other child a paper plate. Use this little rhyme to help reinforce that food is passed to the right. To act it out, the children will pass the plate to their neighbor each time they say, "Pass to the right." When they say, "Stand up," they can stand on their toes. When they say, "Sit down," they can squat.

   Pass to the right,
   Pass to the right,
   Stand up, sit down,
   Pass to the right!

2. Give students the opportunity to politely pass and select their food next time your class is sharing a snack. For example, have students carefully share a plate of cookies. Each student can use their EYES to make their cookie choice and then pass the platter to the student on their right. Tell students the amount of their portion (e.g., one or two cookies, depending on how many you have) and not to take more than their share. Remind students that these behaviors show respect for their classmates who are sharing the meal or snack.

3. Expand the idea of 'politely passing the plate' by helping your students use the same courteous request during the school day. Rather than saying, "Give me a pencil," remind your students of what they learned at the table and to say, "Would you pass me a pencil, please?"

4. Teach students how to pass other food they might share at the dinner table by using a plastic pitcher with a handle and a bowl of peas with a serving utensil. Remind students of the following as they practice passing and serving:

   - The person who is closest to the pitcher is the one who begins passing it to his or her right. Follow the same procedure with the bowl of vegetables.
   - Place the serving spoon in the bowl before passing it.
   - When passing the pitcher, keep the handle toward the person on your right for him or her to grab it (don't hold the handle when passing).
   - Using the serving spoon, carefully scoop one serving and place it on your plate. Remember not to take more than your share!

Chapter 6: Pass the Plate, Please

- When serving yourself, use the serving spoon (not your own spoon) and put it back in the bowl for the next person.
- If you would like something that is not directly in front of you, notice who the bowl or pitcher is closest to and politely say ,"_____, would you please pass the _____?"
- If someone asks for more of something that is in front of you, pass it to them without taking more for yourself (show your selflessness by waiting for it to come back around or asking for it again after the other person is finished).

5. On your "Fine Dining" day, give students the opportunity to prepare for eating in a dining establishment that serves family-style dishes. First, ask students to set the table for you and practice the six steps in getting ready for the meal. Then, have students show you what they have learned about courteous table behavior as they eat their meal. Let students remind each other of what is courteous and discourteous table behavior as they eat and quietly remind students who forget the courteous way to eat at the dining table. Students should politely pass the food to their right, choose their selection with their eyes and not take more than their share. Also, remind students to practice appropriate, respectful conversation with their peers while eating.

Chapter 6: Pass the Plate, Please

Home Connection

Dear Parent/Guardian,

When children learn to respect the needs of others at the table, they naturally begin to demonstrate respect in other areas of life. This week, children are learning how to respectfully pass and select their food at the table. Students are learning the following words of wisdom from Wilbur:

> To choose your bite,
> Look with just your eyes.
> Then pass to the right,
> To show you're wise.

You can reinforce what your child is learning at school by buying or preparing a meal to be served 'Family Style.' Gather your children around the table and ask them to show you what they've learned about politely passing food at the table. Here are some guidelines to help all of you:

- If food is closest to your plate, you should be the first to pass it.
- Pass food to your right (counterclockwise).
- When something is passed to you, make your selection with your EYES and then pick it up with your HAND. Don't touch the other pieces.
- Make sure to keep passing the food, even if you don't want any.
- When passing, keep the handle(s) toward the person you are passing it to for them to grab (don't hold the handle when passing).
- If you would like something that is not directly in front of you, notice who it is closest to and politely say, "_____, would you please pass the _____?"
- If someone asks for more of something that is in front of you, pass it to them without taking more for yourself. Show your selflessness by waiting for it to come back around or asking for it again after the other person is finished.
- The salt and pepper are best friends and always stay together. If someone asks for salt, also pass the pepper.
- If you do not like something that is being passed, try a 'courtesy bite' by taking a small serving. If it is something you can't eat, simply pass it to your neighbor without making a face.

~ From Our Hearts To Yours

Chapter 7

Bread, Buns, Bagels and Biscuits

Materials and Preparation

- Small paper plates (1/student)
- Plastic knives (1/student)
- Napkins (1/student)
- Slices of bread or rolls (1/student)
- Bread basket
- Butter, butter plate, and butter knife
- (Optional) Biscuit or bagel (1 as a sample)

Wilbur's Words of Wisdom

At breakfast, cut;
At dinner, break.
That's how to eat
The bread you bake!

Guiding Children's Learning in the Classroom

Begin by distributing the paper plates, plastic knives, and napkins to students. Remind students to place the napkin in their laps. Lead the following discussion with students:

What are some different kinds of bread or baked goods you might eat for breakfast?
- *Bagels*
- *Biscuits*
- *Banana bread*

When you eat a breakfast bread, such as biscuits or bagels, you should cut or break them open and then spread your butter or cream cheese over one whole side. Then, you take a bite out of it. (Optional—demonstrate how to cut and butter breakfast bread for students.)

With toast, it's the same thing. You butter one whole side and then take a bite. While the toast is still hot, the butter melts nicely when you spread it.

Attributes
Attentiveness, Carefulness

Skills and Objectives:

Children who master the proper rules of bread-eating learn to pay attention to other details in their daily activities and also learn to appreciate the slower pace of eating. In this lesson, children will learn the following:
- To cut and butter breakfast breads
- To break and butter dinner breads
- To gracefully handle "boo-boos" at the table

Chapter 7: Bread, Buns, Bagels and Biscuits

Now, have you ever eaten bread and butter with your lunch or dinner?

- A slice of bread, a roll or a bun are a few different breads you might eat with your lunch or dinner. Do you think you would eat these the same way you eat a biscuit, toast, or a bagel?

- Lunch or dinner breads are eaten a little differently from breakfast breads. You actually are supposed to break off a bite, butter it, and eat that one bite instead of buttering the whole thing.

You are going to get the chance to practice this today. Before you do, however, I'm going to pass around the bread basket and butter dish. Which direction should I pass them?
- *To your right!*

Your serving is one piece of bread. Remember to take only your portion because we want to make sure there is enough for everyone.

When you receive the butter dish, use the butter knife to cut a small piece and place it on your plate—not on your bread. Take enough butter for your piece of bread, but don't take too much. Be careful that crumbs do not get on the butter knife or in the butter dish.

When you have some butter on your plate, you can start eating your bread. (If needed, demonstrate.) Break off one bite-size piece. Then, butter it with your own plastic knife and butter from your own plate. Eat that one piece before breaking another.

Walk around the class to help students properly break and butter their bread.

To reinforce today's lesson, teach students **Wilbur's Words of Wisdom** and the "Bread, Buns, Bagels and Biscuits" song, using the melody of "Ten Little Indians" as a guide.

Bread, Buns, Bagels and Biscuits

Bread, buns, bagels and biscuits,
Bread, buns, bagels and biscuits,
Bread, buns, bagels and biscuits,
  I know how to eat them.

Bread and buns, break and butter,
Bread and buns, break and butter,
Bread and buns, break and butter,
  That's the way to eat them.

Bagels and biscuits, cut and butter,
Bagels and biscuits, cut and butter,
Bagels and biscuits, cut and butter,
  That's the way to eat them.

Chapter 7: Bread, Buns, Bagels and Biscuits

Guiding Children's Learning in the Cafeteria

Focus your cafeteria portion of the lesson on the 'boo-boos' that sometimes happen during meals. During lunch today or later in the week, use the following comments and questions to guide each table in a discussion.

Have you ever reached for something on the table and made a mess? If so, don't be embarrassed; accidents happen to all of us sometimes!

What should you do if you drop a fork or knife on the floor, and you are in someone's home?
- *Pick it up and put it in the sink.*
- *If you are in your own home, excuse yourself while you get another one.*
- *If you are in a friend's home, politely ask for another one.*

> **Definitions:**
>
> **ATTENTIVENESS**
> Carefully watching for ways you can assist others
>
> **CAREFULNESS**
> Respect for your surroundings

What should you do if you drop a fork or knife on the floor, and you are in a restaurant?
- *Leave the fork or knife on the floor, but tell your waiter.*
- *Politely ask your waiter for another one.*

What should you do if you spill some of your drink on the table?
- *Use your napkin to gently pat it dry.*

If you have a major spill, like a glass of milk, apologize to the others at your table and ask for napkins or towels to clean it up.

As you make your rounds, remind students of the following:

- To eat lunch or dinner bread with butter, break off a piece, butter it. Then put that piece in your mouth.
- To eat breakfast bread, spread your butter or jam on the whole thing and take a bite.
- Spills happen to everyone. Just do your best to be careful and help clean it up when you make a mess.
- If you are offered a slice of bread or a roll, only touch the one you are taking.
- Pass bread to the right, just like everything else!
- If someone asks you to pass the bread basket, pass it to them without serving yourself. Wait for the basket to come back around or ask for it again before taking a piece.
- Only take one roll or slice of bread to start. You may ask for another, if you finish yours, and everyone else has been served.

Chapter 7: Bread, Buns, Bagels and Biscuits

EXTENDING
CHILDREN'S LEARNING

1. Lead a discussion with students on other life skills you can learn from preparing just one bite of bread at a time. Use the following examples:

    - *Just as you can't put the whole roll into your mouth at one time, you have to do a little bit of work at a time to complete a big project.*
    - *Buttering a whole piece of bread can be a lot messier than buttering and eating just one piece at a time. Better to keep things clean and simple!*
    - *Buttering and eating one piece of bread at a time can take a while, but it teaches you patience and also gives you more time to enjoy others at meals!*

2. During snack time, 'accidentally' spill your water. Show the children how to politely handle a mishap and how to clean it up. Make sure they realize, however, that accidents are not accidents when they are on purpose. It is not okay to purposefully make a mess, but we should be helpful in cleaning up our own accidents or the accidents of others.

3. Read *Froggy Eats Out* by Jonathan London (2001, Viking Juvenile). This story is a delightful illustration of how to handle spills at the dinner table for all elementary children. It's good, messy fun for everyone.

4. Make sure to incorporate rolls or buns into your next Fine Dining day! Before the meal, ask students to set the table for you and practice their six steps in getting ready for the meal. Have students show you what they have learned about courteous table behavior as they eat their meal. Let students remind each other of what is courteous and discourteous table behavior as they eat, and quietly remind students who forget the courteous way to eat. Students should politely pass the food to their right, choose their selection with their eyes, and not take more than their share. Also, remind students to practice appropriate, respectful conversation with peers while breaking and buttering their bread. If a spill occurs, use it as a learning opportunity to be helpful in cleaning up messes.

Chapter 7: Bread, Buns, Bagels and Biscuits

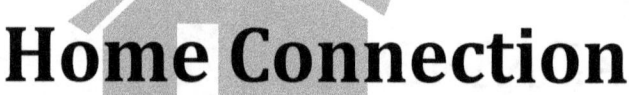

Home Connection

Dear Parent/Guardian,

Breaking bread can teach children valuable life lessons. This week's lesson is on "Bread, Buns, Bagels, Biscuits and Boo-Boos." Children who master the more tedious etiquette of 'bread-eating' learn to appreciate slower meals and to pay attention to details in their daily activities. This week, children are learning the following:

- How to cut and butter breakfast breads
- How to break and butter dinner breads
- How to gracefully handle "boo-boos" at the table

For your next family meal, incorporate dinner bread or rolls to challenge your child on what he or she is learning about breaking and buttering bread. Here are some reminders:

- Lunch and dinner breads, such as bread, rolls or buns, are broken and buttered one bite at a time. You don't need to cut open or butter the entire dinner roll.
- Breakfast breads, such as biscuits and bagels, can be cut open with a knife and spread with butter or jam.
- If the bread basket is in front of you, take a piece and hand it to the person on your right to begin passing it.
- Use your eyes to select your piece and pick it up without touching the other bread in the basket.
- Start by taking only one roll or slice. If you want more and if others have taken their share, you can ask for it to be passed again.
- Cut butter with a clean knife and place it on your plate. Don't touch your bread with the shared butter knife.

Your child is also learning how to gracefully handle mealtime accidents. The next time there is a mess or spill, remind your child of the following:

- Accidents happen to all of us sometimes, so don't be embarrassed.
- If you drop something, put it in the sink and get another.
- If you have a spill, do your best to clean it up and ask for help when needed.

You may know that old adage, "Don't cry over spilled milk." Well, there's a lot of truth in it. Not only should we not cry over spilled milk, but we shouldn't cry out when our children spill their milk. Losing it because our child spills his milk won't keep it from happening again. Having your child assist in cleaning up his mess, however, will teach him important life skills about respecting others around the table. He will also learn how to clean up his own mess instead of relying on others to do it for him.

~ From Our Hearts To Yours

Chapter 8

Spaghetti, Soup and Other Tough Stuff

Materials and Preparation

- Plastic soup bowls (1/student)
- Small plastic plates (1/student)
- Large plastic plates (1/student)
- Plastic soup spoons (1/student)
- Plastic large spoons (1/student)
- Plastic dinner forks (1/student)
- Plastic butter knives (1/student)
- 8" pieces of yarn (3/student)
- (Optional) Dessert spoon (1 as a sample)

NOTE—The cafeteria portion of this lesson is best taught on a day when spaghetti or soup is being served. For other ideas on teaching how to eat various foods, see **Extending Children's Learning** or *Mastering Messy Meals* in the **Appendix** section.

Attributes
Patience, Resourcefulness

Skills and Objectives:

Learning how to eat difficult foods with a few creative rules encourages children to tackle difficult problems with ingenuity—even away from the dinner table. In this lesson, children will learn the following:
- To eat soup without spilling
- To eat spaghetti with grace
- To eat other tough foods

Wilbur's Words of Wisdom

Sip soup from the side,
Twirl spaghetti 'til tied;
No need to be rude
When eating tough food!

Guiding Children's Learning in the Classroom

Begin by distributing the bowls, small plates and soup spoons. For today's lesson, students will be engaged in a role-play to practice eating two different and difficult foods: soup and spaghetti. Teach students how to place their small plate underneath the soup bowl. Have students act out the following instructions as they practice 'eating' soup:

- Who likes to eat soup? Soup is good, but it can be pretty messy, right? Today, we're going to learn how to carefully eat soup when we are eating with others.

- First of all, if the soup is steaming hot, you will want to wait a few minutes before eating. If it's too hot, you might spit it out, which would be gross! Don't blow on the soup, however, because it might blow right out of the bowl.

Chapter 8: Spaghetti, Soup and Other Tough Stuff

- Using your spoon, practice dipping the soup *away* from yourself (Demonstrate). That way, if the soup spills from the spoon right after scooping, it will land in the bowl and not in your lap.

- Practice bringing the spoon to your mouth, rather than leaning over the bowl. I want to see everyone sitting perfectly straight as we practice eating our soup.

- A soup spoon is too large to politely put in your mouth from the front, so you should sip your soup from the *side* of your soup spoon. (Optional—Show a dessert spoon and a soup spoon together, so the children can see the difference.) Practice sipping your soup from the side, but without slurping!

- Leave the spoon on your plate when you're not eating your soup. If you don't have a plate, leave your spoon in the bowl when you're not eating, but be careful that it is steady and won't fall out. Don't place the dirty spoon on the table!

- You can tilt the bowl slightly *away* from you to get the last good drops with your spoon. Tilting it away keeps it from spilling on you.

- When you finish, you should put your spoon on the plate that is under your soup. If there's not a plate underneath, leave the spoon in your bowl.

Now that students have mastered soup, let's move on to spaghetti. Distribute the large plates, large spoons, forks, knives and yarn. Have students create their place-setting with these materials, using their yarn as noodles on their plate. Use the following instructions to teach students how to eat spaghetti:

- Who likes to eat spaghetti? Spaghetti is really good, but it can be pretty messy, right? You are now going to learn how to carefully and politely eat your spaghetti.

- Spaghetti can be cut with a knife or a fork into bite-size pieces before being 'scooped' onto the fork. Show me how you would do this, using your fork and knife.

- Spaghetti can also be eaten by twirling the noodles onto a fork while pressing the fork against a spoon (Demonstrate this for students as they give it a try with their yarn). Keep the tip of the spoon on your plate while pushing the noodles against the spoon. Gently twirl the fork in small turns, until the noodles are wrapped around the fork. It can be tricky at first, but you will get better at twirling your noodles the more you do it.

- You only want to twirl *one* of your pieces of yarn around your fork at a time. Some people try to twirl more spaghetti on their fork than they can fit in their mouths! Make sure you don't have too much on your fork before trying to eat it.

- When the noodles are wrapped neatly around your fork, it's easy to bring it to your mouth without making a mess! When eating real noodles, try not to get the sauce all over your face. If it does get on your face, you can use your napkin to gently blot it.

Chapter 8: Spaghetti, Soup and Other Tough Stuff

Close by teaching students **Wilbur's Words of Wisdom** for a reminder of today's lesson.

Guiding Children's Learning in the Cafeteria

The best reinforcement of this week's classroom lesson will involve giving your students the opportunity to eat real spaghetti, soup or some other difficult food for the cafeteria learning. If spaghetti or soup can be arranged, remind students what they learned in the classroom lesson as you assist them on your rounds through the cafeteria.

(**NOTE**—For spaghetti day, you could add a little fun by giving each student a large spoon to use while eating. Help them practice keeping the tip of their spoon on the plate as they push the noodles against it and twirl their fork. Remind them to keep the spoon on the plate and not be tempted to raise it and lower it as they twirl their fork!)

If spaghetti or soup cannot be arranged, refer to *Mastering Messy Meals* in the **Appendix** section or **Extending Children's Learning** for instruction on how to eat difficult foods that might be served in your cafeteria. Encourage students to think about how to be polite and careful while eating any kind of food. If they don't know how to properly eat a certain food, encourage them to be creative and to do their best.

> **Definitions:**
>
> ***PATIENCE***
> Even-tempered endurance
>
> ***RESOURCEFULNESS***
> Finding creative solutions to everyday problems; using your imagination and mind to re-purpose materials

Chapter 8: Spaghetti, Soup and Other Tough Stuff

EXTENDING
CHILDREN'S LEARNING

1. Give each student a banana, a small paper plate and a plastic knife. Show students how to peel the whole banana and cut it into bite-size pieces before eating. This is the polite way to eat a banana during mealtime; when eating as a snack, it's okay to peel and take a bite.

2. If the budget allows, bring in fresh strawberries with a dip for snack time. Teach students to pick the strawberry up by the stem, dip and eat, leaving the stem on their plate. Remind kids that no one likes it when other people double-dip, as this spreads germs!

3. Next time your students eat chicken in the cafeteria, give them plastic utensils and demonstrate how to eat it with a fork and knife. (You can even do this with fried chicken tenders!) Show students how to stab the chicken with a fork to hold it in place while cutting slices with a knife.

4. Even foods that seem simple enough can be somewhat difficult to eat. A few instructions on how to eat various foods can be found in *Mastering Messy Meals* in the **Appendix** section. Prior to eating one of these meals in the cafeteria, educate your students on how to be respectful of others while eating such foods.

5. Incorporate one or more difficult foods into your "Fine Dining" day. For example, soup can be served as its own course, and spaghetti might be your main entrée. Before the meal, ask students to set the table for you and practice their six steps in getting ready for the meal. Have students show you what they have learned about courteous table behavior as they eat their meal. Students should politely pass the food to their right, choose their selection with their eyes and not take more than their share. Also, remind students to practice appropriate, respectful conversation with peers while properly breaking and buttering their bread. If a spill occurs, use it as a learning opportunity to be helpful in cleaning up messes.

Chapter 8: Spaghetti, Soup and Other Tough Stuff

Home Connection

Dear Parent/Guardian,

Learning how to eat difficult foods with a few creative rules encourages children to tackle difficult problems with ingenuity—even away from the dinner table. This week, your child is learning how to eat difficult or challenging foods, such as soup and spaghetti. Students are being taught **Wilbur's Words of Wisdom**:

> Sip soup from the side,
> Twirl spaghetti 'til tied;
> No need to be rude
> When eating tough food!

This would be a great week and weekend to serve up a few of the more messy foods for practice at home. The whole family will benefit from learning how to tackle eating difficult foods with grace and poise! Here are some pointers on various foods:

- Don't put the whole soup spoon in your mouth, but sip soup from the side of your spoon, without slurping.
- Cut spaghetti with your fork and knife, or twirl one or two noodles on your fork. A large spoon can be used to hold the noodles in place as you twirl. (Remind your child not to twirl more noodles than he can fit in his mouth!)
- If your hamburger is full of lots of good fillings, cut it in half to avoid getting the fillings all over your face when you attempt to take a big bite.
- Hard tacos are eaten with your hands; the way you eat a hot dog. If taco fillings land on the plate, use a fork and not your fingers to scoop them up.
- Soft tacos can also be eaten with your hands; or if the taco is well-stuffed, it might make less of a mess to cut it in bite-size pieces and eat with a fork.
- When eating outdoors, you can eat fried chicken with your fingers. But according to rules of etiquette, fried chicken should be eaten with a fork and knife when served at the dinner table. Place the bones on the edge of the dinner plate.
- At a fast-food restaurant or eating outdoors, you can eat French fries with your fingers. However, fries should be cut into bite-size pieces and eaten with your fork if you're at the dinner table in someone's home or in a restaurant. Put your ketchup on the side (not on the top) of the fries and dip one or two at a time.
- Barbecue ribs can be eaten with your fingers because they're typically served in a casual setting or outdoors. Make sure you have plenty of napkins!
- If corn-on-the-cob is served without holders, you can eat it with your fingers. It's okay to butter the whole ear of corn when it's served hot. It's best to butter the corn as you go, so you don't have butter all over your face as you eat your way down the row of corn.

We hope you have fun learning new ways to eat these favorite foods!

~ From Our Hearts To Yours

Chapter 9

Clear the Clutter

Materials and Preparation

- Plastic forks (1/student)
- Plastic knives (1/student)
- Plastic spoons (1/student)
- Paper plates (1/student)
- Paper napkins (1/student)
- Plastic cups (1/student)

NOTE—You will need two student volunteers to act out a role-play at the beginning of this lesson—one who does a poor job leaving the table and another who is kind and polite when leaving the table. If possible, talk with your volunteers about their roles ahead of time.

Wilbur's Words of Wisdom

Don't be in a hurry to leave the table;
Wait long enough to show you are able.
Ask to be excused and say thank you.
Take your plate to the kitchen,
And then you're through.

Guiding Children's Learning in the Classroom

To begin, distribute plates, cups, utensils and napkins. Ask students to set their place as they have learned in previous lessons. Then, direct the students' attention to your first volunteer. Explain that you are the host and have just had_____ over to your house for a meal. Your first student volunteer should demonstrate a *disrespectful* way to leave the table, exhibiting the following behaviors:

- Her napkin has not been used and is still on the table.
- She jumps up without speaking.
- He leaves his plate, utensils, napkin, and cup on the table.
- He dashes toward the back of the room.

Attributes
Gratefulness, Helpfulness

Skills and Objectives:

Teaching children how to respectfully leave the table supports their development of gratitude. When children pause to say "Thank you" to the one who provided the meal, they learn to be appreciative of those who take care of them. When children clear their plates and assist in clean-up, they learn to be helpful in contributing toward the family. In this lesson, children will learn the following:

- To say "Excuse me," before leaving the table
- To thank the person who provided the food
- To place their napkins on the table (if linen) or in the garbage (if paper) at the end of the meal
- To clear their place at the table
- To help clean the dishes and put away food

Chapter 9: Clear the Clutter

After the first skit, direct the students to your second volunteer. He or she should demonstrate a *respectful* way to leave the table at your house by following these behaviors:

- She has her napkin in her lap.
- She asks, "May I please be excused?"
- He says, "Thank you for my meal! It was wonderful."
- She picks up her plate, utensils, napkin, and cup and takes them to your designated "kitchen."
- He says, "May I help clean up?"

Following the skits, use the comments and questions below to guide students in a discussion:

Which is the better way of acting at the end of a meal in someone's home -- the first skit or the second skit? (*The second skit.*)

What can the first student do differently to be more respectful?
- *He can place his napkin in his lap during the meal.*
- *He can ask to be excused.*
- *He can thank the host.*
- *He can take his place.*
- *He can offer to help clean up.*

Are you practicing the right way or the wrong way of leaving the table in your own home?

Today, we're going to practice our table manners at the end of the meal. We can pretend we have just finished a meal in my home. You can do these same actions at the end of the meal in your own home as well.

- The first thing you do when you finish your food is to place your knife and fork across the center of your plate. The handles should be resting on the edge of your plate, parallel to the table in front of you (demonstrate this for students). This shows your host or your waiter that you are finished and also keeps your utensils from falling on the floor when you, or your waiter, pick up your plate.

- Before jumping up from the table, ask your parent or host if you may be excused by saying, "May I be excused, please?" Practice saying this to your neighbor.

- When your host gives you the okay to leave the table, say something nice about the food, such as, "I enjoyed my dinner," or "You're a great cook," or "Thank you for going to so much trouble." Practice saying something nice about the food to your neighbor.

- Unless you are told not to, you should always take your place setting to the sink after your meal.

- If you have a paper napkin, like you do right now, place it in the center of your

Chapter 9: Clear the Clutter

plate and throw it in the trash when you take your plate to the sink. If you have a cloth napkin, don't fold it or crumple it, but pick it up so it gently folds and place it on the table (Demonstrate this for students with your paper napkin). Never put a cloth napkin on your dirty plate.

- When you leave the table, remember to push your chair under the table before clearing your plate. This makes it easier for others to get around your chair when they are clearing their own plates. Stand and practice pushing in your chair before picking up your plate.

- Whether you are at home or at a friend's house, always offer to help clean up as you take your plate and glass to the sink. If you have food left on your plate, scrape it into the trash and rinse your plate.

Let's make a line in front of the trashcan to practice scraping our 'food' into the garbage. Then we'll step over to the sink and practice rinsing our plates.

Close by reminding students of their meal-end manners that demonstrate gratefulness and helpfulness:

- Place your knife and fork in the center of your plate.
- Ask to be excused.
- Thank your host and say something nice about the food.
- Push in your chair.
- Leave your cloth napkin on the table; throw away your paper napkin.
- Clear your plate by taking it to the sink.
- Scrape food from your plate into the garbage.
- Offer to help clean up.

Definitions:

GRATEFULNESS
Being thankful for those who provide for you

HELPFULNESS
Looking for ways to ease the burdens others carry

Chapter 9: Clear the Clutter

Guiding Children's Learning in the Cafeteria

During lunch today or later in the week, use some or all of the following comments and questions to guide each table of students in a review of what they have learned about table manners:

Should you be silent during the meal, or should you ask and answer questions?
- *Table time is time to talk!*
- *Be polite by answering questions and coming up with questions to ask.*

When do you put the napkin in your lap?
- *Right after sitting down*

How long does the napkin stay in your lap?
- *Until I leave the table*

If someone asks you to pass the salt, how do you do it?
- *The salt and pepper are best friends and always stay together.*
- *If someone asks for salt, I should pass the pepper with it.*

Fill in the blank: Food should be passed to the (RIGHT).

Who should be the one to start passing the food?
- *The person whose plate is closest to it*
- *The person who does not have to reach over someone to get it*

Fill in the blank: You choose your piece by using your (EYES).
- *Touch only one piece, your own.*

What should you do if you do not like something that is being served?
- *Take a small serving anyway to try a 'courtesy bite.'*
- *If it is something I can't eat, say, "No thank you," or pass it on without making a face.*

Fill in the blank: Don't talk with your mouth (FULL).

Why is it not a good idea to talk with your mouth full?
- *It is gross for the other people around you to look at.*
- *It is easy for food to accidentally fly out of your mouth, which is also very unkind to the people eating around you.*
- *You might choke on your food.*

Fill in the blanks: Sit (STRAIGHT), don't (SLOUCH) and (SMILE)!

Chapter 9: Clear the Clutter

How should you eat bread and butter at the lunch or dinner table?
- *Break a piece, butter it and eat it.*
- *Don't butter the whole thing all at once.*

Show and tell me how you eat spaghetti.
- *Twirl it with your fork.*
- *Cut it in bite size pieces.*

Show and tell me how you eat soup.
- *Sip it from the side of your spoon.*
- *Don't slurp.*

Where do you keep your utensils while you are eating?
- *When I am not holding them, I place them on the top edge of my plate.*

Where do you put your fork and knife when you are finished? Show me.
- *In the center of my plate, with the handle resting on the edge of my plate.*
- *Parallel to the table, in the center of my plate.*

What do you say before you stand at the end of the meal?
- *May I please be excused?*
- *Thank you!*
- *The food was wonderful!*

What should you do with your plate after you finish eating?
- *Scrape my food into the trash.*
- *Take it to the sink.*
- *Rinse it with water.*
- *Put it in the dishwasher.*

Assist students who need help while making your rounds through the cafeteria.

Chapter 9: Clear the Clutter

EXTENDING CHILDREN'S LEARNING

1. Let Wilbur get in on the fun this week. Tell students that Wilbur is hosting their meal at snack time. Tell them they have an opportunity to show Wilbur all they've learned. After snacks are finished, remind students to tell Wilbur "Thank you" for providing their food and to ask to be excused. Allow them to take their plate to the trash or pretend they're rinsing it and putting it in the dishwasher.

2. Tell students they're going to practice their 'meal-end-manners' in the cafeteria. Ask them to thank the cafeteria staff and to compliment the food when receiving their tray. Have students ask to be excused from the table and to push in their chairs before clearing their places. After scraping the leftover food from their trays into the trash can, remind students to again say "Thank you" to the cafeteria staff when taking their trays to the correct place for washing.

3. Use the following rhyme, set to the tune of "The Ants Go Marching," to help students practice the end-of-the-meal steps:

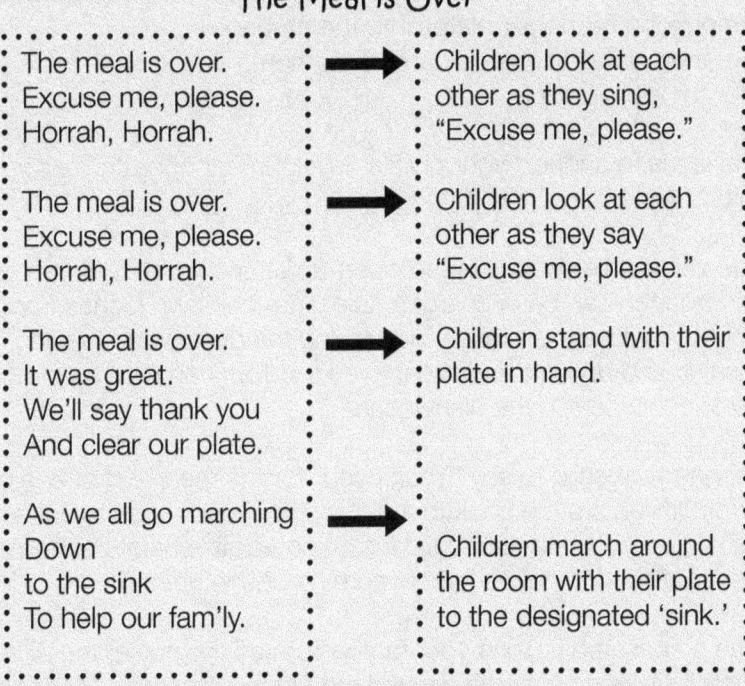

The Meal is Over

The meal is over. Excuse me, please. Horrah, Horrah.	Children look at each other as they sing, "Excuse me, please."
The meal is over. Excuse me, please. Horrah, Horrah.	Children look at each other as they say "Excuse me, please."
The meal is over. It was great. We'll say thank you And clear our plate.	Children stand with their plate in hand.
As we all go marching Down to the sink To help our fam'ly.	Children march around the room with their plate to the designated 'sink.'

4. Have students practice their meal-end manners in concluding your "Fine Dining" day. Before the meal, ask students to set the table for you and practice their six steps in getting ready for the meal. Have students show you what they have learned about courteous table behavior as they eat their meal. Students should politely pass the food to their right, choose their selection with their eyes and not take more than their share. Also, remind students to practice appropriate, respectful conversation with peers while properly breaking and buttering their bread. If a spill occurs, use it as a learning opportunity to be helpful in cleaning up messes. At the end of the meal, make sure they say "Thank you," "Excuse me" and help clear their plates.

Chapter 9: Clear the Clutter

Home Connection

Dear Parent/Guardian,

Teaching children how to respectfully leave the table supports their development of gratitude. When children pause to say 'Thank you' to the one who provided the meal, they learn to be appreciative of those who take care of them. When children clear their plates and assist in clean-up, they learn to be helpful in contributing toward the family. In this week's lesson, children are learning what to do when the meal is done.

Students are learning the following:

- To place their knives and forks in the center of their plates when they finish eating.
- To ask their parent or host to be excused.
- To thank the person who provided their food.
- To say something nice about the food (e.g., "This was really good!").
- To push in their chairs when they leave the table.
- To throw away their paper napkin, but leave their cloth napkin on the table.
- To scrape food from their plates into the garbage.
- To take their plates to the sink and rinse them.
- To offer to help clean up.

Here are some ideas to support your child's development of gratitude for meals and helpfulness after meals:

- Include children of all ages in the clean-up after a meal. Children as young as kindergarten can be in charge of clearing their own dishes from the table. Elementary children can take turns rinsing the dishes and loading the dishwasher, or washing and drying the dishes. Even toddlers can help by placing plastic cups, plates or containers in the dishwasher!

- Encourage your child to say "Thank you" for the meal and offer a compliment to the cook. (If you are the cook, gently remind your spouse to set a good example of this!) When you help your child form appreciative habits at home, these habits will become second nature everywhere he or she goes!

Make mealtime a treasured ritual in your family. Turn off the noise, the distractions and the outside world. Make dinner a time when the family gathers to hear about each other's day, to share happy news and sad news and to deepen their commitment to each other and to the family.

Remember, families who sit together at the dinner table will stand together when trouble comes!

~ From Our Hearts To Yours

Chapter 10

Restaurant Rules

Materials and Preparation

- Copies of "Billy's Bistro" Menu (1/student)
- Paper plates (1/student)
- Paper napkins (1/student)
- Forks (1/student)
- Knives (1/student)
- Spoons (1/student)
- Manners of the Heart® apron
- Small notepad
- Pen or pencil

NOTE—Before you begin today's lesson, be sure to put on your apron for taking your students' orders!

Wilbur's Words of Wisdom

Try not to wiggle.
Try not to giggle.
Keep elbows at your waist
And always take a taste.
Please don't be lazy.
Say "thanks" like crazy.
Then you'll have lots of fun
When it's all said and done!

Guiding Children's Learning in the Classroom

Attributes
Participation, Respectfulness

Skills and Objectives:
Teaching table manners at home and at school prepares children for respectful dining in public places. In this lesson, children will learn the following:
- To respectfully order their food
- To be considerate of other diners by speaking quietly
- To exercise patience as they wait for others to finish their meal
- To thank the adults who serve and pay for their meal

Give students their place-setting materials and ask them to set their places. Then ask your students to line up at the door of your classroom. Welcome your students to 'Billy's Bistro.' Ask the boys to seat the girls. Remind the girls to thank the boys.

Give your students a menu after they take their seats, and ask them to look over the menu selections.

Now, walk the children through the ordering process with these reminders:

- When you are seated at the dinner table, whether at home or in a restaurant, what is the first thing you should do?
    - Place your napkin on your lap!

Chapter 10: Restaurant Rules

- Now, look over your menu to decide what you would like to order. Decide what you want to eat quickly because no one likes to wait long before ordering.

- Ask an adult what you are allowed to order. Don't let your eyes get bigger than your stomach! Order only what you can eat.

- I'm going to come around the room to take your order and when I do, I want to hear you speak clearly and see you looking in my eyes. You should do this for the waiter when you are in a restaurant as well. This is what you should say, "I would like to have the _____, please."

Go around the room taking the order of each student so they can practice respectfully and maturely placing their order. If time allows, take their drink order as well. Pretend to jot down their selections on your notepad just as a waiter would do. Afterwards, use the following questions to guide students in a discussion about respectful restaurant behavior:

Show me how you should act while waiting for your food in a restaurant. (Remind them to practice the following.)
- *Talk in an inside voice*
- *Sit straight—not slouching*
- *Stay seated*
- *Not move all around*
- *Not put elbows on the table*
- *Not play with the ketchup, sugar, salt or pepper*
- *Participate in the conversation*

What are some things to remember when the food comes? (Help them with the following.)
- *Notice if the waiter is trying to set food or drinks down and make room for him or her.*
- *Say "Thank you!" to the waiter.*
- *Wait until everyone is served before you begin eating.*
- *Keep your napkin in your lap with the top flap folded down by one third and use the top third to clean your mouth or fingers.*
- *Don't talk with your mouth full.*
- *Don't eat too quickly or make a mess.*
- *Only say good things about the food on your plate.*
- *Eat a 'courtesy bite' of food you have not tried to see if you will like it.*

What are some things to remember at the end of the meal? (Help students with the following while having them act out their suggestions.)
- *Wait patiently for everyone to finish eating.*
- *Place your knife and fork (and spoon, if it has been used) across the center of your plate so the waiter knows to take them.*
- *Gently lift your napkin—don't fold it—and place it in the center of your place at the table (but not on your plate, if it is still there).*

Chapter 10: Restaurant Rules

- *Thank the person who paid for your meal.*
- *Thank the host or hostess when you leave the restaurant.*

Thank the children for coming to 'Billy's Bistro' and tell them it has been a pleasure to serve them!

Close by asking students what they have learned about eating in a restaurant. Some possible responses:
- *Put your napkin in your lap as soon as you're seated.*
- *Ask an adult what you are allowed to order.*
- *Don't order more than you will eat!*
- *Decide quickly what you want to eat.*
- *Speak clearly and look the waiter in the eyes when ordering.*
- *Talk in an inside voice.*
- *Sit straight and don't move all around.*
- *Don't put elbows on the table.*
- *Participate in conversation.*
- *Say "Please" and "Thank you."*
- *Try a 'courtesy bite.'*
- *Wait patiently for everyone to finish.*

Definitions:

PARTICIPATION
Choosing to be fully involved in the task or project at hand

RESPECTFULNESS
Treating others with dignity

Chapter 10: Restaurant Rules

Guiding Children's Learning in the Cafeteria

During lunch today or later in the week, have students pretend they are eating their lunch in a restaurant. Ask the boys to seat the girls. Remind them to use all their table manners, including using an inside voice, and to thank the cafeteria staff with a smile and a compliment on the food!

Use the following comments and questions to guide each table in a discussion:

What is something you might do to occupy your time while waiting for a table at a restaurant? (No electronics allowed!)
- *Listen to the conversation of adults.*
- *Play games with others while you wait, such as, "I spy" or "First Letter."*
- *Talk about your day.*
- *Say hello to others passing.*
- *Look at a menu to decide what you are going to eat.*

Do you like to put your elbows on the table? Why do you think it is important NOT to put your elbows on the table?
- *Makes you sleepy, so you don't participate in the conversation.*
- *Might make your sleeves dirty.*
- *Spreads germs on the table.*
- *Makes it hard for others at the table to see around you.*
- *Makes it hard for you to see others (e.g., others at the table or the waiter).*

Do you ever get bored while you're waiting for others to finish their meal? What is something you can do while waiting for others to finish eating?
- *Think of questions to ask and ask them when it is quiet.*
- *Play a quiet game (e.g., "I Spy") with your brother or sister.*

Have you ever ordered something in a restaurant that you did not like? What would be the polite thing to do if you don't like something that is on your plate?
- *Don't complain or make a face.*
- *Try to eat it anyway—you may like it!*
- *Try to eat it anyway—this is how you will learn to like different foods.*
- *Try to eat it anyway out of respect for the person who cooked your meal and the person who is paying for your meal.*
- *Eat the other things on your plate that you do like.*

As you make your rounds, remind students of the following restaurant 'rules':
- Put your napkin in your lap as soon as you're seated.
- Talk in an inside voice.
- Sit straight and don't move all around.
- Don't put elbows on the table.
- Participate in conversation with others at your table.
- Say "Please" and "Thank you."
- Try a 'courtesy bite' of everything on your plate.
- Before standing, wait patiently for everyone to finish.

Chapter 10: Restaurant Rules

EXTENDING
CHILDREN'S LEARNING

1. *Mrs. Piggle Wiggle* books by Betty MacDonald are classics filled with stories that still delight children today while teaching lessons that children don't readily learn from us! One such story is "The Slow-Eater-Tiny-Bite-Taker." Mrs. Piggle Wiggle comes up with a creative solution to this age-old problem with children. We highly recommend it as a fun and informative read for encouraging your students to be respectful of others at the table.

2. Watch for opportunities to use the lessons learned at the table in other areas of your students' day. Remind your children that table manners involve putting the needs of others ahead of their own—something they can do on the playground, in the classroom and at home. Let them practice this skill of serving others in small ways. For example, they can allow classmates to go first in the drinking fountain line!

3. Remind students that even the seemingly 'silly' table manners have a purpose! For example, teach students what to do with plastic or paper garbage (e.g., cracker wrappers or straw paper) when dining at a restaurant. Most people put their paper or plastic trash in the center of the table, but this makes it difficult for the waiter to keep the table clean of trash. That is why the 'rules of etiquette' teach us to put any wrappers at the edge of the table, so the wait staff can reach down and pick up trash without disturbing the meal or reaching across diners at the table.

4. Serve students as if they are in a restaurant on your "Fine Dining" day—better yet, conclude your table manners curriculum by treating your students to a real restaurant experience! If the budget or time is limited, do your best to re-create the restaurant environment in your classroom or cafeteria. Treat your students by setting the table for them. Remind students to practice their six steps in getting ready for the meal and have them show you what they have learned about courteous table behavior as they eat. Students should politely pass the food to their right, choose their selection with their eyes and not take more than their share. Also, remind students to practice appropriate, respectful conversation with peers while properly breaking and buttering their bread. If a spill occurs, use it as a learning opportunity to encourage being helpful in cleaning up messes. At the end of the meal, make sure they thank their servers!

Chapter 10: Restaurant Rules

Home Connection

Dear Parent/Guardian,

Teaching table manners at home and at school prepares children for respectful dining in public places. After ten weeks of lessons, your child is now learning how to apply his or her knowledge of table manners in a restaurant environment! Children are learning the following:

- To respectfully order their food
- To be considerate of other diners by speaking quietly
- To exercise patience as they wait for others to finish their meal
- To thank the adults who serve and pay for their meal

One of the intentions of this curriculum is to enhance your family's ability to connect at mealtime by teaching elementary children the importance of table manners. In case you're not convinced, here are a few reminders of the benefits of the family dinner table:

- Your kids will snack less, helping them to form healthy eating habits.
- You and your child have the perfect setting to share the daily occurrences in each other's lives *every day*.
- You'll learn about your child's problems before they become issues.
- According to research, your child will get better grades in school and have a more positive attitude about his or her future.
- Talking to your child will help prevent them from getting involved with negative behaviors like drinking alcohol, taking drugs or smoking.
- Finally, research indicates that meal time is a more powerful influence on children than time spent in school, studying, church, playing sports or art activities.

To get your family excited about dinner together, why not set up an at-home restaurant? Welcome your child to your restaurant just like a host would do, showing them to their seats. If you have sons and daughters, remind the boys to seat the girls for dinner! Rather than passing out a menu, recommend the nightly special (whatever you've prepared for supper). Remind your child of the lessons being learned at school:

- To put your napkin in your lap as soon as you're seated
- To ask an adult what you are allowed to order
- To not order more than you will eat
- To speak clearly and look the waiter in the eyes when ordering
- To talk using an inside voice
- To sit straight and not wiggle
- Not to put elbows on the table
- To participate in conversation
- To say "Please" and "Thank you"
- To try a 'courtesy bite'
- To wait patiently for all to finish

We hope *Manners of the Heart At the Table* has helped your family learn about much more than just table manners!

~ From Our Hearts To Yours

Chapter 10: Restaurant Rules

Billy's Bistro

Appetizers
Gracie's Green Salad
Wilbur's Hot Wings
Good-Hearted Grapes
Peter's Pumpkin Soup

Side Orders
Bully's Beans
Considerate Carrots
Friendly French Fries
Honest Onion Rings

Sandwiches
Buddy's Burgers
Polly's PBJ
Chelsey's Cheeseburgers
Helen's Ham & Cheese

Entrees
Tripper's Trout
Respectful Ravioli
Cheerful Chicken
Freddy's Fish Sticks

Desserts
Penelope's Pudding
Humble Pie
Forgiveness Fudge
Carolina's Cheesecake

Beverages
Polite Punch
Sweet Tea
Manners Milk
Happle Juice

Appendix

MASTERING MESSY MEALS 81
ACTIVITIES AND ATTRIBUTES CHART 82
MATERIALS CHART 83
WILBUR'S GLOSSARY 84

MASTERING MESSY MEALS

Some foods have different rules for eating, depending on where you are dining.

Fried Chicken:
- Fried chicken should be eaten with a fork, if you're eating at the dinner table.
  - Hold the piece of chicken with a fork, cut the meat away with a knife. Stab the piece of chicken meat to eat.
  - Place the bones on a separate plate or on the edge of the dinner plate. Don't leave the bones in the center of the plate.
- At a picnic or outdoors, you may eat fried chicken with your fingers.

French Fries:
- French fries should be cut into bite-size pieces and eaten with your fork if you're at the dinner table in someone's home or in a restaurant. Put the ketchup on the side, not on top of the fries, and then dip one or two at a time.
- When eating at a fast-food restaurant or outdoors, you may eat your french fries with your fingers.

Messy Foods:
- Barbecue ribs are eaten with your fingers because they are typically served in a casual setting or outdoors.
- If you eat a banana as a snack, peel it as you bite it. If you're eating a banana at the dinner table, it should be peeled, cut into bite-size pieces and eaten with a fork.
- If corn-on-the-cob is served without holders, you may eat it with your fingers. It's okay to butter the whole ear of corn when it's served hot. It's best to butter the ear as you go so you don't have butter all over your face as you eat down the row of corn.

Some foods have different rules for eating, depending on how they are served.
- If bacon is crispy, you may eat it with your fingers. If bacon is a bit limp, it should be cut into bite-size pieces and eaten with a fork.
- Fresh fruit cut into pieces should be eaten with a fork, not your fingers.
- Strawberries that are served with a dip, like chocolate or sugar, can be held by the stem and dipped. Eat the berry up to the stem and place the stem on your plate. (No double-dipping!)

Some foods need a little help before putting them in your mouth.
- If your hamburger is full of lots of good fillings, cut it in half to avoid getting the fillings all over your face when you attempt to take a big bite.
- Hard tacos are eaten with the hands, the way you eat a hot dog, from one end to the next. If taco fillings land on the plate, use a fork, not your fingers to scoop them up.
- Soft tacos may also be eaten with your hands or if the taco is well-stuffed, it might make less of a mess to cut it in bite-size pieces and eat with a fork.

Activities and Attributes Chart

Chapter	Lesson Title	Attributes	Game	Activity sheet	Role Play	Song/Cheer	Props	Puppets
1	Table Talk	Participation, Respectfulness	•				•	
2	Flatware Goes Somewhere	Appreciation, Helpfulness, Orderliness		•	•		•	
3	Come One, Come All	Gratitude, Politeness		•		•	•	
4	Mess Hall Manners	Consideration, Courtesy			•		•	•
5	Tools of the Table	Carefulness, Self-control			•		•	
6	Pass the Plate, Please	Awareness, Selflessness, Sharing			•		•	
7	Bread, Buns, Bagels and Biscuits	Attentiveness, Carefulness			•	•	•	
8	Spaghetti, Soup and Other Tough Stuff	Patience, Resourcefulness			•		•	
9	Clear the Clutter	Gratefulness, Helpfulness			•		•	
10	Restaurant Rules	Participation, Respectfulness		•	•		•	

Materials Chart

Ch.	Lesson Title	Materials Needed
1	Table Talk	• Bean bag or soft ball (1 or more)
2	Flatware Goes Somewhere	• Copies of "Place-Setting Map" (1/student) • Plastic forks (1/student) • Plastic knives (1/student) • Plastic spoons (1/student) • Paper dinner plates (1/student) • Paper bread/salad plates (1/student) • Paper napkins (1/student) • Plastic cups (1/student)
3	Come One, Come All	• Brightly colored napkins (1/student)
4	Mess Hall Manners	• Wise Ol' Wilbur puppet • 1 plate • 1 fork • 1 napkin
5	Tools of the Table	• Plastic forks (1/child) • Plastic knives (1/child) • Plastic spoons (1/child) • Paper plates (1/child)
6	Pass the Plate, Please	• Paper plates (1/student) • Slices of bread, rolls or crackers (1/student) • Bread basket(s) (1/circle of students) • Salt and pepper shakers (for Cafeteria learning)
7	Bread, Buns, Bagels and Biscuits	• Small paper plates (1/student) • Plastic knives (1/student) • Napkins (1/student) • Slices of bread or rolls (1/student) • Bread basket • Butter, butter plate and butter knife • (Optional) Biscuit or bagel (1 as a sample)
8	Spaghetti, Soup and Other Tough Stuff	• Plastic soup bowls (1/student) • Small plastic plates (1/student) • Large plastic plates (1/student) • Plastic soup spoons (1/student) • Plastic large spoons (1/student) • Plastic dinner forks (1/student) • Plastic butter knives (1/student) • 8" pieces of yarn (3/student) • (Optional) Dessert spoon (1 as a sample)
9	Clear the Clutter	• Plastic forks (1/student) • Plastic knives (1/student) • Plastic spoons (1/student) • Paper plates (1/student) • Paper napkins (1/student) • Plastic cups (1/student)
10	Restaurants Rule	• Copies of "Billy's Bistro" Menu (1/student) • Paper plates (1/student) • Paper napkins (1/student) • Forks (1/student) • Knives (1/student) • Spoons (1/student) • Manners of the Heart® apron • Notepad • Pen or pencil

Wilbur's Glossary

A

ACCEPTANCE
Treating everyone you meet with the same respect, regardless of differences

APPRECIATION
Recognizing and acknowledging value in people, places and things

APPROPRIATENESS
Knowing the right thing to say or do in any given situation

ATTENTIVENESS
Carefully watching for ways you can assist others

AWARENESS
Open eyes and an open heart to the needs of others

C

CAREFULNESS
Respect for your surroundings

CITIZENSHIP
An attitude of cooperation and social responsibility

CIVILITY
To respect others and self for the betterment of community

CONSCIENTIOUSNESS
Diligent carefulness

CONSIDERATION
Taking into account the feelings of others before you speak or act

COOPERATION
Working with others for everyone's best; choosing to be helpful, not hurtful

COURTESY
Gentle kindnesses shown others

E

EMPATHY
Walking in another person's shoes

ENCOURAGEMENT
Offering words to others to build their confidence

EXPRESSIVENESS
Revealing the content of your heart

F

FRIENDLINESS
Welcoming others by offering a quick smile and a kind word

Wilbur's Glossary

G

GENEROSITY
Gladly and willingly giving your time, your talent, and your treasure

GENTLENESS
Speaking and acting with tenderness

GOODNESS
Being kind, compassionate, and forgiving

GRACIOUSNESS
Being courteous, understanding, and generous in all situations

GRATEFULNESS
Being thankful for those who provide for you

GRATITUDE
Appreciating what you have

H

HELPFULNESS
Looking for ways to ease the burdens others carry

HONOR
Valuing the worth of another by showing respect

HOSPITALITY
Serving others with the purpose of making them feel cared for and comfortable

HUMBLE CONFIDENCE
The courage to be your best so that you can help others become their best

HUMILITY
Not caring who gets credit

K

KINDNESS
Showing care and consideration in an unexpected and exceptional way

L

LOVE
Genuinely caring for another, unconditionally

LOYALTY
Faithful devotion

M

MANNERS
Treating others the way you want to be treated

MATURITY
The ability to make the right choice in spite of negative influences

O

OBEDIENCE
Choosing to submit to authority

Wilbur's Glossary

ORDERLINESS
Keeping the space around me neat and tidy

P

PARTICIPATION
Choosing to be fully involved in the task or project at hand

PATIENCE
Even-tempered endurance

PATRIOTISM
Loving our country enough to protect it and the principles upon which it was founded

POLITENESS
Using kind words and actions in all situations

R

RESOURCEFULLNESS
Finding creative soultions to everyday problems; using your imagination and mind to repurpose materials

RESPONSIBILITY
Following through on your duties without supervision

S

SELF-CONTROL
The ability to manage yourself when no one is looking

SELF-ESTEEM
Self-absorption presenting itself as self-conceit on one extreme and self-consciousness on the other

SELF-RESPECT
A character trait which comes from treating others with dignity

SELFLESSNESS
Choosing to give of yourself with no expectation of return or consideration of loss

SHARING
Offering the best you have to others

SPORTSMANSHIP
Being more concerned with supporting your team than helping yourself

T

THOUGHTFULNESS
Looking for ways to make others feel loved

TRUSTWORTHINESS
Doing what you say you're going to do when you say you will do it

U

UNDERSTANDING
Looking at others and listening to others without judgment

Manners of the Heart® is a non-profit organization working to create a more positive moral culture and bring back respect, responsibility and civility to our society. At Manners of the Heart®, we are dedicated to transforming homes, schools and communities through instructional programs designed to build character, strengthen morals, and increase respectfulness among children and adults. This character education, referred to as "Heart Education," is the training of the next generation to have not only head knowledge to lead, but heart knowledge to lead in the right direction.

MANNERS of the HEART®
215 Royal Street
Baton Rouge, Louisiana 70802
(225) 383-3235
www.mannersoftheheart.org

www.mannersoftheheart.org

Without respect...
schools cannot educate.

At Manners of the Heart®, we don't tell children they're great, we help them become great. We don't tell children they're the best, we help them become their best. We don't teach children to do the right thing for a reward, but to do the right thing because it's the right thing to do. The outcome—their self-esteem is replaced with self-respect and self-control. Through our elementary curriculum, schools experience a rise in academic scores, a decrease in disciplinary actions and an increase in parental involvement. Students develop respect for others and self-respect, creating a classroom environment conducive to teaching, enabling them to become all they are meant to be. Visit our website for more information on how you can bring Manners of the Heart® to your school.

www.mannersoftheheart.org

Without respect... parents cannot parent.

In our competitive world, many parents are raising their children in child- and parent-centered environments. Rather than turning out disciplined, caring, productive, respectful and well-mannered children, they are often undisciplined, rude, greedy, disrespectful and ill-mannered. Jill equips families to raise children who are respectful, engaged and motivated in a character-centered home. She addresses current challenges, offering "preventive parenting" to help parents avoid attitude and behavior issues prevalent in today's society. Contact Manners of the Heart today to schedule a dynamic parent seminar or conference to make a lasting impact on your community.

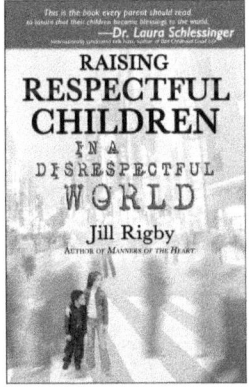 

www.mannersoftheheart.org

215 Royal Street | Baton Rouge, Louisiana 70802
Phone: 225.383.3235 | www.mannersoftheheart.org